EVENINGS IN ALBANY

A ROOM IN ALBANY (1938)

From a painting by Stella Bowen, by permission of Miss Bowen and Messrs. Collins, Publishers, Ltd.

Evenings in Albany

by

Clifford Bax

London
Eyre & Spottiswoode, Ltd.
14, 15 & 16 Bedford Street W.C.2

First Published . . . *1942*

BOOK
PRODUCTION
WAR ECONOMY
STANDARD

THIS BOOK IS PRODUCED IN
COMPLETE CONFORMITY WITH THE
AUTHORIZED ECONOMY STANDARD

PRINTED IN GREAT BRITAIN FOR
EYRE AND SPOTTISWOODE (PUBLISHERS) LONDON

To
MEUM STEWART
who has perceived that life is a story
to which the soul is listening

CONTENTS

I

THAT IVORY TOWER

ON a summer's afternoon about fifteen years ago, Martin Shaw, Doctor of Music, and I, Doctor of nothing, paused at that point where Vigo Street becomes Burlington Gardens, and looked in at the wide many-paned window of the Bodley Head. We began, very naturally, to talk about the 'nineties, and the brilliant scandalous Yellow Book which had been launched from the Bodley Head; of Beardsley, Wilde, Dowson, absinthe and sin, Baron Corvo (the old rascal) and hansom-cabs, the Diamond Jubilee, the promenade at the Empire, and Mr. Rudyard Kipling.

Then we looked upward at the window above the Bodley Head, a window exceptionally tall, ample in width and gracefully convex.

"I wonder," mused my friend, "I wonder who lives up there, on the other side of that noble window? It's a part of Albany, you know, and somehow or other I've always had a hopeless passion for Albany." Strolling onward just a few steps, we came to the north entrance of that old aristocratic preserve, and looked down a long, gabled arcade, but we also noticed a hanging board upon which these minatory words had been painted,

PRIVATE, NO THOROUGHFARE

However, the beadle who ought to have thrust us away with contumely (for we were only a couple of artists), happened not to be on duty, and Shaw said, "Let's go through. They can't eat us. Now, this long, covered passage," he continued, as we tried to look aristocratic, "is, I believe, called 'the Rope Walk.' Some old admiral first gave it that name. . . ."

Seven years later I was living in those rooms above the Bodley Head at the wide main window of which Martin Shaw and I had gazed so reverently: and it is because I was happier in Albany than in any of my other London dwellings that I am going to write this book. I wish it were possible to offer the reader a drink or a smoke, or the two together, while we consider the flavour of a period (only yesterday, as the clock measures) which vanished away so abruptly.

II

Even in 1932 Albany was, I suppose, an anachronism; and in varying degrees we who lived there—we Albanians—must also have been anachronisms: but since it is possible that the reader does not quite know what I mean by "Albany," let me explain that it is a private estate (with a private arcade) in the very centre of London's West End. It runs parallel with Sackville Street and with Bond Street, and comes about midway between them. Consequently its arcade ("the Rope Walk") connects Piccadilly with Burlington Gardens.

At the Piccadilly end, opposite Hatchard's incomparable bookshop, stands the courtyard and "the Mansion." The "mansion" is an immense but unlovely palace, built in 1770. It was built for Lord Melbourne and his wild little wife who threw herself so recklessly at Byron. Twenty years later, they exchanged houses with the Duke of York, one of George the Third's many sons—in fact, that very Duke who stands on his tremendous Column, trying (how vainly) to compete with Nelson. Bad luck at cards made the Duke a bankrupt in 1798, and he had to dispose of his palace and of the long, slender garden which connected the palace with Vigo Street and Burlington Gardens. In 1800 (Keats was five years old, Shelley was eight, Wordsworth was prematurely mature at thirty), an enterprising syndicate bought the estate and, building that celebrated stone-tiled arcade, set up to right and left of it the earliest of all London flats. They may be called "rooms" or "chambers," but they are really the distinguished first-begetters of all the millions of flats in London or, indeed, in Great Britain.

These "chambers in Albany" have been cited in many plays and many novels as the most elegant of all possible backgrounds for the disillusioned husband, the idle lord, or the fastidious bachelor. Raffles ("the amateur cracksman") was said to live in Albany just so that his secret career as a burglar might seem the more inappropriate, the more startling. A few of those who live in Albany may deal in Stock Exchange "margins," but none of us could conceivably have picked a mere pocket. Then, too, Byron dwelt there for a short while—months only—before his misery-burdened marriage; and Gladstone spent seven of his early and solemn years as an Albanian; and here lived Bulwer Lytton, that industrious and learned nobleman who even acquired a notable knowledge of occultism. He had recognised the intimidating significance of "the Dweller on the Threshold." Do you know what it means?

The buildings date from a period of dignified architecture, but Albany, except for a few details, is not a monument of beauty. It would not be too much to say that the "enterprising syndicate" to which I have referred seems—with remarkable enterprise—to have forestalled the tasteless commercialism which in England was to take the place of architecture for a hundred years from, shall we say, eighteen-forty. The style is monastic. In some chambers you may find impressive but quite false panelling. And if we wish to observe the living conditions of the servant-class during most of the nineteenth century, we may inspect the Albany basements. They are now either vacant or used as lumber-rooms. In my basement I found one minute window close to the ceiling, and a massive kitchen-range that dumbly bore witness to the use in Victorian times of that unpardonable dungeon. If servants in Albany had to endure such conditions, what, I wondered, can have been the condition of the less exalted?

So late as the 'nineties, Albany was still a settlement of privilege and distinction. An aged Albanian who had lived there for sixty years told me, on Coronation Day, when all of us uncongealed a little, that "forty years ago we rode on horseback into Piccadilly, and the police would hold up the traffic for our cavalcade." In those days, too, and right up to the beginning of the Four Years War, no women were allowed to live in Albany. Up to the present time no child has outraged those bachelor traditions by being born within cry of the Rope Walk. This, then, was a remnant of Nelsonic London and a lingering stronghold of pomp and circumstance. The entrances at each end were guarded by beadles in gold-braided top-hats and brown surcoats with scarlet lapels—formidable figures who not seldom acrimoniously scolded errand-boys for whistling within their domain.

I took the rooms which are numbered "G2," and I need not describe them in full because this has already been done with his usual expertness as a reporter by Arnold Bennett in *The Pretty Lady*. He must have admired, as I did, the large living-room which was eighteen feet high and had, as the reader knows already, so broad and lofty a window. I doubt if Bennett made much use of the balcony outside that window, for it looked as though I were the first inhabitant of "G2" to train creepers along those rusty old railings. It was odd to be living in the centre of London, an extraordinary sensation to wake up in the West End. I felt as though I, a lifelong Londoner, could now understand how London feels to a foreigner: and this almost-unreal or after-death-like experience was intensified when on my first morning, awakened by the early traffic, I went out on to the little balcony, and saw the pigeons pretending that the ledges of Savile Row were the rocks from which their wild ancestors had flown. I had, moreover, to acquire a new technique of sleep. Revellers in the summer of 1932 drove their cars homeward at high speed and usually hooted just under my bedroom window. They continued to do so until about three in the morning. At five in the morning, all the year round, a horse-drawn cart, carrying vegetables to Covent Garden, went clip-clop, clip-clop along Vigo Street, and within half an hour a new procession of cars began: but after a few months I hardly heard them at all and was only sometimes awakened by the elderly man and wife as they jogged on their way to market.

III

It is not the men of action or even the men of affairs who charge a writer with "escaping" (from reality) if he does not treat of the present. The man of action or affairs is himself only too pleased, as a rule, if he can sometimes escape from the immediate. The charge emanates from our self-called "intellectuals," and we may well be surprised that they should repeat it so often. We may also be surprised by their persistent description of a detached mind as dwelling in an "Ivory Tower," for we might suppose that this architectural impossibility would irritate a sensitive imagination.

Some of them have already expressed dissatisfaction with Miss Austen because she entirely disregarded the Napoleonic peril, although most sensible persons will be thankful that her work is not burdened with the dead wood of old politics. But how is it possible that our very "intellectuals" cannot perceive, as we do, that throughout recorded history the arts have provided an alternative to the anxieties of war, politics, or business and have been, to use another word, a recreation. The art-loving princes of the Italian Renaissance can hardly be said to have lived in Ivory Towers; and it would be equally foolish to maintain that Botticelli, Perugino, and Titian infused their work with the turbulent spirit of the ages in which it was produced. On the contrary, they ignore what was to them the Present, nor, in fact, is it easy to think of a single first-rate work of art, in painting or in literature, which is excellent by reason of its connection with contemporaneous affairs. Homer was telling an old story, and the dead bits in Dante's poem are those which were merely topical.

The essential value of art is precisely that it upholds the uncontemporary interests of man, and so offers a recreation from an over-tense and near-sighted absorption in the practical and the immediate. It is to the mind what open air is to the body; and those who declare us to be guilty of "escapism" if we do not write about newspaper matters might as reasonably upbraid the man who sometimes goes for a morning swim or plays a set or two at lawn-tennis. Art is, in short, the highest form of human relaxation from the strain of real life; and writers who refer to escapism and the Ivory Tower have mistaken their calling. They should have been Trades Union leaders or professional politicians.

Here, then, is my Apologia. Europe is on fire—yes, but not for ever; and it is better not to meddle at all if we cannot give any practical help.

II

THE BEAUTIFUL AMERICAN

OUTSIDE the big curved window which overhangs Vigo Street there was a stone balcony with iron railings. These railings were not so much weather-beaten as weather-eaten, and this made me surmise that they probably dated from 1800, the year in which that part of Albany was built. Moreover, a few weeks before the Coronation Procession of King George and Queen Elizabeth I used to notice a suspicious figure prowling about on the farther side of the narrow street and peering up at my big window. True, I had carefully trained a Virginia creeper across the greater part of the railings, and I had even a vine—presumably the only vine-tree in the parish of St. James—so that it was just possible that this man was admiring my enterprise: but one day he called upon me, and said that he was an Inspector of Buildings. He had observed, as I too had observed, that from this little balcony I should be able to get a momentary glimpse of the Procession as it passed along Regent Street; and he now told me that my balcony had been put there merely for ornament and that, if I proposed to use it, he must ask me to place metal struts under the old stonework. Then I knew for certain that the balcony was indeed a remnant of old London.

When I first was in those rooms it proved to be a most amusing grand-stand, especially on spring and summer evenings. The street-walking harlots in this neighbourhood were, I suppose, the Upper Ten in their branch of harlotry, and for two or three summers I was pleased and amused to watch them: pleased, because they dressed stylishly, walked with a charming provocation and, seen from the balcony, looked astonishingly pretty; and amused, as I said, because of their technique, their use of toy-dogs, their tendency to linger under the street-lamp, the elaborately disinterested glance at any motorist who began to slow down, the colloquy through the window of the car,

6

and (it may be) the superb contempt with which the girl would walk away if the man did not mean business. The girls had a quadrangular beat. They paraded along Piccadilly, up Bond Street, round by Burlington Gardens and Vigo Street, and down to Piccadilly again by way of Sackville Street. All of them seemed to be friends, and it was obvious that if your pal looked like doing a little business, you melted away towards Bond Street or sometimes up Savile Row. Very often they hunted in pairs, and inevitably I soon came to know most of them by sight. Indeed, I invented names for them. There was, for example, the Caterpillar who, even in midsummer, dressed herself tightly in green velvet; and Mrs. Slammekin, a strapping wench and probably what is termed in the trade a disciplinarian; and the Marquise who, though in her early twenties, had achieved the miracle of getting her hair dyed silver. As a rule these elegant girls did not need to walk for long, and by midnight they had been replaced by a much inferior brew. In the small hours Vigo Street sometimes became Hogarthian. The quarrels under my bedroom window were often so vitriolic as to wake me, and once, putting on a dressing-gown and going to the balcony, I discerned a trollop lying dead drunk in the gutter, and watched while one of her sisters bundled her into a crawling taxi-cab and so sent her home.

This privileged view of the preludes to sin considerably excited two or three young novelists of my acquaintance, but I quickly discovered that the spectacle had an even livelier interest for most women. There was, for example, Lady Mynk who, in my youth, had been one of the loveliest women on the London stage. I had met her, after a good many years, at some conference in Oxford, and no sooner had I told her about Mrs. Slammekin, the Caterpillar, and the Marquise than she insisted on being invited to dinner. This made me ponder. Perhaps every woman is a wanton, a worshipper of wild natural forces, and capable of riding away on a broomstick to a rocky solitude or a wild place in the woods where she may forget all the absurd constraints of civilisation; but women like Lady Mynk have to burn their broomsticks when they marry, and it seemed to me that they wanted to watch an exhibition of unrestrained sexuality. Those girls down there in the street were free to do so many things which Lady Mynk had always had to resist.

So she came to dinner on a fine evening of July. I could hardly restrain her impatience. "There's very little to see," I said, "before about nine o'clock. Take a chirping glass . . . a drop of sherry: and have your dinner, upstairs, and then we will come back and see if we can spy the Caterpillar."

"And the Marquise?" she asked.

"And Mrs. Slammekin, and all of them," I promised, and with this assurance she accepted a cigarette. In due time we went upstairs and ate our dinner, but conversation was of the clodhopping kind, and I had to tell her that eight out of ten prostitutes, at least in my part of London, were French, and that on Bank Holidays they deserted their ordinary beats. Why? On those days the West End is almost empty. But where do they go? Well, I asked one of them, and she said, "In the parks."

Eventually, we came downstairs again, and giving Sarah her handsome "wrap," I took her on to the old balcony. We were lucky enough to see the Caterpillar, but only once, and Mrs. Slammekin twice (after which she vanished into a car), but unfortunately the Marquise must have had a previous appointment. However, it was all I could do to get Lady Mynk away from that balcony, and I do not know that I should have succeeded if she had not felt a slight waft of nocturnal coldness. Then she returned to the tall room and arranged herself statuesquely in the largest of my arm-chairs. She looked considerably like the Tragic Muse, and suddenly she said, "Who is the loveliest woman you've ever seen? I'm not asking for a compliment. Who was she—really?"

My memory streamed back over fourteen or fifteen years. At that period I was living a happy Bohemian life in a vast studio at a negligible rent, and it would be hypocritical to pretend that I was indifferent to the grace and charm of women. Now, I cannot remember how I came to know her, but there was then a rich old lady, mad about music, who lived in a historic house on the border of Palace Green—ten minutes' walk from my studio. I cannot guess why she troubled to encourage my visits, for I was no musician, and she—old Mrs. Neustein—had not much interest in literature. Still, there it was—from time to time she would ask me to dinner at eight o'clock, and in this way I met with somewhat arrogant young poets from impoverished Germany, with several young actors who hoped that Mrs. Neustein would set them up in management, and with many of her musical chickens: but I am now thinking particularly of one night in the rainless, parched, magnificent summer of 1921. I remember that, having just finished a play, I had spent the afternoon at the Oval where the scorched turf had the colour of light corduroy, and that coming back to the studio I found one of my old friend's attractive invitations. It was much better, certainly, to bath, change into evening attire, and enjoy a long, luxurious dinner with glasses of Rudesheimer, in Mrs. Neustein's mansion than to prise open a tin of pilchards, hew bread and cheese, and draw a glass or two of lime-juice and water.

And so it came about that, walking slowly down Kensington High Street (slowly, because those summer evenings never had time to cool) I duly arrived at the large, long house; and as the butler adopted my hat, stick, gloves, and scarf, I heard somebody playing in the manner of Busoni on Mrs. Neustein's Bechstein Grand. When, however, I came into the drawing-room, which was delightfully cool because gay awnings had protected the windows all the long day, I perceived with astonishment that all this rapture of sound was being produced by an invisible master—that, in fact, I had been listening for the first time to an electrical pianola. I shall not forget those two or three minutes in the twilight before my hostess appeared, for it seemed to me that I had walked into a story from the Arabian Nights and that there never could be anything more wonderful than to hear magnificent music passionately interpreted by the ghost of some Olympian pianist. Our sense of wonder, you should realise, had not then been calloused by familiarity with the marvels of the radio-djinn.

Well, the other guests arrived, some four of them, and we sat down to our leisurely and expensive dinner at a round table of walnut-wood, which was probably itself a museum-piece.

One of the guests was a writer of whom I had vaguely heard, a stoutish self-confident man, about ten years older than I; and I can still experience the chill which crept over my ambitious brain when he observed, complacently, "As we grow older, we learn our limitations. I mean, you and I now recognise that we are not, and never could be, the equals of Shakespeare or Dostoevski . . ." This defeatist attitude was, I thought, very poor-spirited.

And so, with pleasant interchange of views upon the Russian Ballet as it had been in 1913 and as it was in 1921; with an attempt to assess the importance of Goethe, Mrs. Neustein's demi-god; with sips of old brandy, and with two or three of the Preludes exquisitely floated into the gathering darkness by perhaps the wraith of old Pachmann, all of us were uncommonly happy when the minute-hand of the Louis-Quinze clock moved over the point of half-past nine. Mrs. Neustein, however, considered that, even so, we were not happy enough; and I admit that I should now agree with her that in respect of happiness we should always pile Pelion upon Ossa.

"Listen, children," she exclaimed, "it's a lovely night. Let's drive up in the Daimler to Hampstead and call on the Thoroughgoods. They'll interest you," she added, turning to me, "they believe in the soul."

She pressed a bell-button, and a footman emerged from somewhere in the bowels of Kensington. The chauffeur was then aroused from his shirt-sleeved study of the starting-prices and, ignoring the Morris-Cowley, he brought the Daimler to the front door. I must admit that we were not sorry to get into the open air, even although it was somewhat jaded by the three months' drought.

Then we drove through the greater part of respectable and attractive London—all the mounting way from the lowlands of Kensington to the heights of Hampstead. And there is, I always feel, a rarefied pleasure in being carried to some unknown destiny. That, it may be, is why since puberty "I have been half in love with easeful death." . . . At least I shall maintain that it was fun to be carried onward and upward, through that hundred-and-fifteenth night of the Rainless Summer, to an eighteenth-century house, visited in their own day by Addison and Swift, and to find myself in the bosom of one of those Hampstead families which somehow managed to reconcile a passion for culture with an evangelical observance of Mosaic morality.

I am not much of a talker because, knowing already the contents of my own mind, I am naturally more interested in discovering the unknown thoughts of other people; and in consequence I was left to myself for the best part of fifteen minutes. And then—then she came in. . . .

"Who?" asked Sarah Mynk, who was never quick in the uptake.

"The loveliest girl," I replied, "whom I'd ever seen."

"Tell me about her."

"But, Sarah," I protested, "could you make me realise the emotion which you, as a brilliant and highly cultivated woman, felt when you first saw the Parthenon; or when first, as a small child, even more attractive than you are to-day, you came upon cowslips in all their April merriment; when first you heard some God-gifted tenor in a Puccini part; or when first you watched the eternal sun rise up again out of the eternal sea? No, no, my dear Sarah—we cannot convey the emotional harmonics which mean almost everything in what, without them, would be common experience."

"Still," persisted Sarah, not a little jealous, "was she dark or fair (fair, I suppose), tall or small? You can tell me that!"

She was dark. She was tall. Her figure was faultless; her eyes were long and lustrous; and her features had been moulded by God in one of those moods when He forgets about mathematics, allows the universe to run on upon its own momentum and is intent solely upon creating beauty. Who was she? An American, and she had the amusing soft drawl of the cultivated New Yorker. I could not catch her name—but then I never do catch names. Our hostess, putting this lovely girl beside me, whispered, "She's only seventeen. Niece of the great American conductor, Ludwig von Kammerlein." So I tried to talk with the marvellous American about music; but she was an incarnation of all poetry, of all that captivates our youthful

2

fancy in Keats, in Tennyson, in Rossetti, so that I could not help thinking, "At last I have found that Isis of the Egyptians, that Iseult of the Troubadours, that Princess from Far Away, that avatar of romantic womanhood, for whom all true men for innumerable generations have been seeking and longing." Our hostess, perceiving, as she supposed in her tactful way, that the girl was boring me, came up to us and said, "Show him your bed, dear. It's rather beautiful," she added, turning to me, "——a cinque-cento Florentine four-poster."

The girl rose, and as I followed her out of the long living-room and up the stairs, I felt exactly as though I were associating with Helen of Troy or even with Phryne—who was probably the more entertaining. Even to say this, however, is not enough, for my American added to superb beauty a look of romance which is absent from the loveliest faces of the antique world.

We went into her room. "Here is the bed," she said softly, "and it really is rather lovely, don't you think?" I looked at the fine carving, the delicate painting, of that old Italian four-poster, and it made me realise that at one time in the world's history people had regarded beauty as something of which you could not possibly have too much. For a moment I wondered wildly whether our hostess might, after all, have had designs upon our virtue, and whether the same thought was hovering in my companion's mind; but she merely gave me a friendly smile, and we went downstairs to the others.

"I don't believe that it ended there," observed Lady Mynk.

"Not quite," I admitted, "but it was fourteen years before I heard anything more about her. "

"And you mean to say you remembered her all those years?"

"Yes. She had a beauty you couldn't forget."

"And when *did* you hear of her?"

"The day before yesterday. . . ."

It was true. An American lady had written to say that she was introducing "a charming girl whom I think you'll like. Her name is Gloria Menzil, and she's one of our most famous mannequins." Miss Menzil arrived—a tall and splendid type of New York night-club beauty. She was about five-foot-ten in height, and she amused me by saying, as we stood by my mantelpiece, "Say, you're so tall, you make me feel good. You make me feel like a piece of Dresden china."

During lunch I discovered that Miss Menzil took a keen delight in modern music. "And then, Sarah," I said, "I asked her if she could give me any news of the most beautiful girl whom I'd ever seen. An American," I told her, "though of course that hardly means that you must inevitably know her. She was staying in Hampstead with some people named Thoroughgood—oh, fifteen years ago. All I can tell you is that she was related to the conductor Ludwig von Kammerlein. She took me upstairs to see her bed, a fine piece of Florentine work."

Gloria Menzil answered softly, "My dear, I'm that girl."

III

THE HAPPIEST OF ALL MEN

LIFE would be a tedious and crude experience were it not for the quickening society of women: and yet, as every intelligent woman is aware, we men do need at times to squander an evening upon ourselves: and perhaps it is in winter that these Viking-assemblies, not uninspired by the modern equivalent of mead, can be most enjoyable. Elegance, in which woman excel, may suit the months of spring: romance, the keynote and essence of femininity, blooms during summer as unthinkingly as the rose; in September, too, a visit from a woman may have the backward-looking charm of the first autumnal fire in the grate: but women should hibernate in winter or wing their beauty away as the swallows do. A winter night is at war with silks and satins and bare shoulders, and with all those fine differences which make a fair woman so fascinating to a man. A winter night is, on the contrary, an accompaniment in the right key to an exclusively male dinner-party. A man-and-woman friendship needs constant attention: a friendship between man and man is, on the contrary, a warm, graceless, comfortable igloo—from which it will be difficult to lure the one man or the other.

And such a male-party I had arranged. My guests were to be three, for I had found that if there are more than four persons at a dinner-table the conversation disintegrates. A. D. Peters was there, a man so astute and implacable that he ought to have been at the head of the New York police; and Hugh Prew, an expert chemist, a fine cricketer, a skilled player of the clarinet; and Eric Gillett, who seems to have read every book which has appeared since the days of Caxton, who delights equally in wine, wit, and wisdom, and who is the very type and embodiment of the steadfast friend.

Having finished our dinner in the small upper-room, we clattered down the narrow staircase and settled ourselves in the arm-chairs of the tall and pale green living-room. This room was, in fact, the salient feature of G2 Albany. It was almost three times my own height, and I am, admittedly, no dwarf. Knowing their tastes, because I had known all of them for a tidy bunch of years, I handed large globes of brandy to Peters and to Gillett, and provided Prew, as I provided myself, with a not ignoble whisky-and-soda. All of us, moreover, appreciated the Casteneda cigars which, in those happier days, I had carefully matured.

In due time our talk alighted upon the theme of "happiness." What conditions, we began to wonder, are necessary if a man is to be uncommonly happy? And is it possible, I ventured, to name any one man whom we could accept as having been the happiest man who has ever lived?

I had started a nimble hare. As one essential of happiness, Hugh voted for health; but Eric Gillett put in the demurrer that Robert Louis Stevenson, one of our gayest writers, was always a sick man. Peters proposed that much depends upon a man's period. "Hardly anyone," he submitted, "can have enjoyed life in the Dark Ages, except perhaps a few barons: and there was no fun in being a black man on the coast of West Africa before the slave-trade was abolished." For my part, I suggested that fame or success ought not to be overlooked and that it must be delightful to achieve renown when you are young enough to enjoy it. "But," said Eric, "if a man outlives his fame, as Drinkwater did—what a wearisome anti-climax! No—I shall vote for a comfortable income and an harmonious love-life."

You can see that we now stood upon the brink of that exciting question—who was the happiest of all men? It goes without saying that we had to exclude hypothetical or anonymous candidates, as, for example, medieval monks at work upon illuminated manuscripts (for they may have had their secret sorrows) and Indian yogis who, for all that we could know, may have existed in a state beyond pleasure or pain, or the lazy and unambitious hedonists of Bali or Tahiti.

For some time we assessed the claim of Saint Francis of Assisi: one of us maintaining that you cannot be happy until you care quite as much about other people as about yourself: but Peters, reacting against so perilous a dose of mysticism, plumped for a more material self-fulfilment. He advanced the claim of "Alexander the Great, successful beyond all probability, and a man who died young—but not too young!"

Then they asked me to name my candidate. Famous artists and luckily beautiful women rushed pell-mell through my imagination. I considered Raphael, Lady Hamilton, and Mozart, Charlie Chaplin, Ellen Terry, and Noel Coward. I pondered the ecstasies of Santa Teresa, the serene mind of Socrates, the genius and the fecund home-life of Sebastian Bach. I thought of the versatile Xenophon; but, as usual, wavered so long that before I had come to any decision the others had left me far behind. And I heard Hugh saying, significantly, "After all, it must be extremely pleasant never to bother yourself about philosophy or religion or even politics, and just to take the world as it is. . . ." We were converging, like rival explorers of the Arctic, upon the personality of W. G. Grace, and the more closely we inspected his life, the more certain we became that we had at last found The Happiest Man Who Ever Existed.

His good fortune began with the very date at which, as the poet AE would have said, he "entered into Outer Things." He was lucky to be born an Englishman in 1848. Society, ominously rocked by the waves of the French Revolution as they rolled against the cliffs of Albion, had settled down again; Napoleon was a harmless historical effigy: and England was just upon the brink of a period of wealth and peace and prosperity which would endure for some sixty years. In the seventies and eighties of the Victorian century a young man with no more than three or four hundred a year could live like a nabob. Now, W. G.'s father was a successful West Country doctor, and the young man, although he would have to choose a profession, was comfortably removed from the horrors of Victorian poverty. As for health, who ever heard that W. G. had even a common cold?

Again, these advantages might have counted for less if the boy had been born in London or Liverpool or Leeds. His headquarters, on the contrary, were in Gloucestershire, and this meant that he was familiar with that unspoiled Wessex of seventy and eighty years ago which glows for ever with the loveliness of a long September sunset in the prose-romances of Thomas Hardy. Grace himself was probably a robust Philistine. We know, for example, that he advised a young cricketer to keep away from books if he wished to see a cricket-ball clearly. But experience makes me confident that the green charm of Gloucestershire and Somerset must have enriched him with unacknowledged delight. Indeed, it is pleasant to hear that this West Countryman never lost his local accent and seemed in consequence, to carry a sense of cornfields and thatched roofs and medieval barns into the grimiest centres of industry and even into the stiff-necked pavilion at Lord's.

Old Dr. Grace (let me tell or remind you) had a big orchard in his garden, and within this orchard there was clearance enough for a cricket pitch. Here it was, then, that the Grace clan—father and uncles and boys—disported themselves whenever, in the comfortable eighteen-sixties, they had time for a game. So great was the father's delight in cricket that he founded "The West Gloucestershire Cricket Club": and little Gilbert Grace first played for his father's new club at the green age of nine. We may surely presume that Dr. Grace must, that morning, have been "one short." And seeing that the infant was repeatedly pitted against enormous adults, we cannot be surprised that he was twelve years old before he scored his very first fifty. But then, growing taller and brawnier, he is chosen in 1864 (at the ripe age of sixteen) to play against "The Gentlemen of Sussex." These gentlemen must have made a smoky and wearisome journey in the—as it were—top-hatted railway-trains of that era. To score a hundred runs was, in those days, a feat so rare that we can only liken it to the discovery of a Queen Anne farthing: and yet, on a rustical wicket and against the speed-bowling which was then fashionable, our eupeptic and robust young Gloucestershire lad astonishes the cricket world by scoring 170 in his first innings and 56 not out in his second. Lillywhite, a mid-Victorian forerunner of the august Wisden, might well have said something more prescient and more handsome than that "he promises to be a good bat, bowls very fairly": but the critic who can instantly recognise a John Keats must himself have a dash of genius.

Two years later, this "good bat" weighed twelve stone, stood six-foot-one, and had the shoulders of Hercules. Not only did he score many centuries, he dumbfounded the sporting world of 1866 by actually scoring double centuries: and already at the age of eighteen, young Grace was an attraction to the public wherever he happened to play. When at last, in 1869 this famous young man came of age, the *Daily Telegraph* observed: "Not only is Mr. Gilbert Grace the best batsman in England: it is the old story of the race—'Eclipse' first, the others nowhere." Even Raphael, even Mozart, even Noel Coward, could not claim at so early an age such a fairy-story success. Consider, too, how in 1876 he amazed his contemporaries by making scores of over three hundred, figures which in those days must have seemed almost incredible: and remember, too, that throughout the long midsummer of Victorian peace and plenty, Grace, moving onward from the twenties to the thirties and thence again to the forties, continued to play that boys' game, wearing his boyish cap, and bowling and fielding with all the excitement of a thirteen-year-old at a prep. school. The moralist might object that Grace excelled only in a game, and that grown men ought to put away childish things. It is true, no doubt, that he was a gigantic Peter Pan and that his long, full life was a prolongation of all that is jolliest in boyhood; but, if it comes to assessing happiness, what other man, I wonder, could trump his claim?

His marriage was happy, and his wife bore him sons. In the winter he practised his profession of surgery. In early years he was a fine runner; throughout his life he was a skilled shot and an ardent fisherman; and owing to his pre-eminence as a cricketer he was able to travel without expense in Australia, Canada, and the United States. Even in middle-age, despite his formidable girth, W. G. still over-topped all rivals in the cricket field, and as a personality he was probably better known throughout England than even Mr. Gladstone or Mr. Disraeli. In 1895, at the age of forty-six, he amazed all cricketers by scoring a thousand runs in the month of May: but how many cricket-lovers realise, I wonder, that in 1902, when he was fifty-four, "the Old Man" bowled more successfully against the visiting Australians than any other English bowler? He continued to play that game which he first learned in a Gloucestershire orchard until he was close upon sixty. There were, I admit, a few sorrows to fleck that large, robust, and fortunate career. Grace must have been saddened by the early death of his brother "G. F.," and, later, by the even more untimely death of his son, "young W. G.": and in the last months of his life, "the Old Man," we are told, was considerably upset by the Zeppelin raids of 1915.

Nevertheless, I believe we were right. I believe that no man has been happier than this fabulous representative of mid-Victorian success. Think once again of all his good luck! Robust health, early and enduring renown, a happy marriage, a sufficient income, a life which covered a long stretch of English history at its most prosperous and serene, and not the faintest infection of Hamlet's melancholy but, on the contrary, the temperament of a complete and satisfied extrovert—is there anything which can be added to these ingredients in a prescription for human happiness?

Soon after eleven, the knocker on my front door announced the arrival of an unexpected visitor. Mrs. Phyllis Vallance, with a pleasant young escort, had come on from a play at the Haymarket: and when I had given her a nightcap and all of us were back again in our chairs, I told her the result of our deliberations: but, as I had expected, she would have nothing to do with a mere cricketer. She put forward the claims of Pasteur and Lister. And yet, when the evening was over and I was getting into bed, I found myself still thinking of that simple and triumphant life.

IV

THE PARTY AND THE POET

I MARVEL that no man has written a comedy about the extent to which we are moulded by our servants. There was, for example, Lady Sycamore, who bestrode London like a colossus, planting one foot in the business world of the City and the other among the skylights of Chelsea. She took a studio in Chelsea with my pretty, amusing, and talented friend—Jocelyn Villiers—and here they proposed to entertain their lovers. Martha Sycamore had no pleasure in roughing it. She needed somebody to bring her a pre-breakfast cup of tea, to lay the table, to wash up; and so she engaged a couple, reputed to be man and wife. It was obviously necessary that the couple should go out of the studio for at least one evening in the seven; but they proved to be such devoted home-birds that, after strolling up and down the Embankment for some forty-five minutes, back they came—the noise of their latch-key gravely agitating the quartet at their picnic supper in the studio. Martha, not to be daunted, presented the couple with expensive tickets for the local cinema, but the Man and Wife, once they were inside the picture-palace, quickly decided that their courting days were over and that they would sooner spend their time in the little kitchen, he with his evening paper, she with her knitting.

Unless there was now to be an end of all amorous experiment, which was not to be thought on, Martha and Jocelyn (who told me the story) would need to put their heads together and somehow solve the great Servant Problem. "I can't order them to stay out of the studio for three hours every Thursday," lamented Lady Sycamore. "And they're such jewels," murmured Jocelyn, who would sooner have remained celibate than have to wash up. Then Martha's eye glittered. "I have it," she cried, "there shall be service and there shall be sin!"

On the next morning Martha had a heart-to-heart talk with the cook, explaining how deeply she had become interested in the soul-developing systems of the East and how eager Miss Villiers was to improve her own spiritual state. "If meditation is to be fruitful," said Lady Sycamore, "absolute quiet is imperative. I am not saying that you and George are noisy. On the contrary, I have sometimes not even heard your latch-key in the lock. But we must keep the vibrations clear—the vibrations. I suggest, therefore, that on Thursdays you and George should visit my old housekeeper in Highgate and stay with her until, shall we say, eleven o'clock? It's not very far to Highgate. You can easily get there in forty minutes."

Even so, a few unforeseen difficulties remained. The champagne bottles which provided a prelude to meditation might, at a pinch, be hidden behind books or canvases, but it was not so easy to dispose of some sixty oyster-shells. "So what did you do?" I asked of Jocelyn. "Well," she replied, "*her* boy packed the bottles into one suitcase, and *my* boy packed the shells into another. Then they tipped the gutted shells and the gilt-necked bottles into the dustbins of our nearest neighbours."

I, too, have been shaped by my housekeepers. The first whom I had in Albany not only wore dark spectacles, but saw life through them: an iron Scot whose conception of virtue was more stringent than my own, and so it was that I lost her. An ancient, sweet-natured Irishwoman, originally a Dubliner, replaced her, as cowslips in due time replace the icicles of February. So far as I can now remember, her name was Cathleen ni Hoolihan, and certainly I was continually adapting a famous line and murmuring, "I saw an old woman and she had the walk of a queen"—aye, and the manners! Fifty years earlier they must have been saying:

> Young she is, and fair she is, and would be crowned a queen,
> Were the King's son at home here with Kathaleen-Ny-Houlahan.

But her heart was weak with the strain of years, and when a handsome Jewess, a very Delilah, distributed gas-masks in Albany, the dispossessed Queen of Ireland succumbed to panic, packed her boxes, and fled to her native land.

I, suddenly wrecked on that desert island in Piccadilly, and being much less handy than my prototype Robinson Crusoe, then wildly engaged Mrs. Freitag: a loquacious and lachrymose hoyden of forty-seven. Within a few hours of our meeting I had realised that she was the unluckiest and the hardest-used woman in Great Britain and yet, nevertheless, the kindest, the most forgiving, the most self-sacrificing. No one, I gathered had ever done so much for other people. Her husband, a Jewish undertaker, had fled from Hitler and now from herself. Gifted with a genius for cleaning the flat, Mrs. Freitag had not even the tenderest talent for cooking. In answer to an ultimatum I had confessed that I liked welsh-rarebit, and all my meals for a month triumphantly ended with Mrs. Freitag's version of that humble dish. This might have mattered little, since I am no Petronius about food, except that I have never shared Jehovah's delight in burnt-offerings.

Freitag had, of course, her likes and dislikes among my visitors. I cannot remember that she expressed enthusiasm about any of the women, not even about Jocelyn, but certainly she had her favourite among the men. She had chosen the same man whom Cathleen ni Hoolihan had once chosen.

Now that he is tossing down sherries in a Better World, there can be no harm in saying that Mrs. Freitag made a special favourite of the poet Dick Bridport. Is it not strange to think that the name of Keats or of Shelley looked, a hundred years ago, as unfamiliar as the name of Bridport looked when his first book appeared in nineteen hundred and five? And have you reflected, I wonder, upon the queer fact that great poets are seldom named by diminutives even among their closest friends? Why did everybody call Bridport "Dick" or "Dicky," and did it reveal some flaw in his equipment? I cannot hear Milton's mother calling for "Jacky," or Spenser's wife referring to "Eddie." Actors may speak of "Old Bill," but who dared call Tennyson "Alf" or Dante "Ally"?

Dick Bridport was now close on sixty, and he was no common or garden drinker. He was a collector's piece. He disdained no form of alcohol and has been known to mingle beer with vodka, Château Yquem with whisky. He stood head and shoulders above all other drinkers, not excluding orchestral horn-players, and, had he lived a few years longer, would have become the acknowledged G.O.M. of the Bacchic world. More than once have I seen him sit down after breakfast with a book to review and a bottle of whisky at his elbow, and, sure enough, within sixty or seventy minutes the bottle and the review would be simultaneously finished. I remember, too, how some of his friends, fearing that he would write no more poetry unless he abandoned the bottle, persuaded him to be overhauled by a friendly doctor who himself wrote facetious ballades: but to the chagrin rather than the relief of those good Samaritans, the doctor had to present the sodden poet with a clean bill of health.

Why was it that Freitag made such a fuss over my extravagant friend? I do not believe that women wanted to reform or even to mother him. I believe that my housekeeper liked him for the very quality which had aroused so much affection in me. Despite his failings—particularly his insolence when he was flown with wine—Bridport loved humanity and loved it in detail. He had almost the medieval outlook which regarded any and every man as an imperishable soul, and all of them as equal in value. Mrs. Freitag was just as real to him as the Cabinet Minister with whom, perhaps, he had been dining. Moreover, he was tireless in helping young writers and seemed always to be befriending gaol-birds, fellow-drunkards, and distressed damsels. He did, however, raise the problem of how far we ordinary folk must put up with the uncomfortable aspects of genius. Wagner was an unscrupulous woman-grabber;

Ernest Dowson disdained the use of toilet-paper; Simeon Solomon went so far as to burgle his friends' houses; but the sorely tried contemporary who does not stay the course may expect to frizzle in the frying-pan of posterity. Fond of the poet as I was, even I had to draw the line at putting him up for the night. If he were sober there might be no danger in his practice of chain-smoking in bed, but as a rule the danger of fire in the flat would have been considerable.

Within a few weeks of her first welsh-rarebit Mrs. Freitag contracted a fixed idea that I ought to give a cocktail-party. I told her that I hated cocktails only a little less than I hated parties, and that I had lived for seven years in those rooms without giving a party and proposed to go down to my grave with that record intact. The truth is that I dislike a crowd because I so greatly like each separate person, and that I detest a babel because I am at a disadvantage in a shouting-match. Few subjects of conversation can be interestingly shouted. Freitag, however, when she was not reciting her unexampled misfortunes, returned again and again to her darling project. I put up a stern defence. For three weeks I withstood her, sometimes even sinking to inquiries about her health in order that she might forget the party. At last there came a morning when I was preoccupied with some prose which had got into a tangle and, not having the patience to repeat my part in our daily dialogue, I exclaimed irascibly, "Very well, Mrs. Freitag, we'll have your party on Tuesday next." And when I had finished my work for the day I chose from my address-book the twenty persons whom I liked best.

Hardly had I written down her name when Jocelyn Villiers rang up. In her charming and erratic way she had decided to give me a present—"something," she said, "that was destined for Albany, something that will make you think of dark ringlets and 'The Keepsake.'" And so the next day, determined not to inflict welsh-rarebit upon her, I took Jocelyn to the Automobile Club and there we had lunch, a lunch gaily garlanded, as it were, with witty and exotic scandals. As for her gift it was indeed charming—a wicker-work basket in faintly yellowing china, so characteristic of the giver that when I placed it on the mantelpiece of my dining-room I seemed almost to possess a fragment of Jocelyn's dainty and amusing personality.

Freitag's party, as we called it, was, I imagine, not greatly different from most other parties. It was certainly of no importance, for neither politics nor rank was represented at it. The guests had, however, been chosen for beauty or for brains, and this in defiance of certain women-friends who used, not without complacence, to rebuke me for not knowing any plain women. They regarded this fact as a demonstration of my spiritual backwardness, but I maintained that as a rule the better-looking a woman is the better will her companionship be. The apex of the party was achieved, no doubt, with the arrival of Commander C. B. Fry who, not content with Nature's magnificent endowment, appeared triply superb in the dark dignity of his naval uniform. For the rest, everyone was surprised that Freitag herself should seem to take no interest in this party of her own contrivance, and should remain in the kitchen from beginning to end of it. And of course everyone commented on the absence of Dick Bridport. "It means that the drinks will go round," said one. "The first party for years," commented another, "at which Dicky has not insulted anybody." "Or have you at last given him up?" asked a third. The truth was, however, that he had suddenly and vehemently adopted the cause of two Indian terrorists who were soon to be executed for blowing up a post office near Simla.

Charles Fry is, I think, the only good and copious talker of my acquaintance who miraculously manages not to repeat himself; and on this occasion, as on many another, he was the strongest magnet in the assembly. When he left, there was a kind of long, lingering twilight as in little groups of two or three my picked companions went out into London in search of dinner.

I had only the not unpleasant task of tidying up the relics of three delightful hours, and I remember thinking what a stupendous drink, what a world-shattering cocktail, might be compounded from the residue of sherry, benedictine, vodka, gin, and Grand Marnier which gleamed at the base of those bottles.

The room was heavy with smoke, and since there was almost an hour to my dinner-time, I went for a walk round the ducks in St. James's Park, thinking of all the pleasant spirits who had convened at Freitag's party; and when I returned to the flat, Mrs. Freitag, sticking out an obstinate underlip, said grimly, "Mr. Bridport rung up. 'E's in a state. Something about the Empire. I told 'im to have supper with you and to stay the night."

"But, really!" I protested; "you know perfectly well that I don't wish to put him up. It isn't safe."

"Poor man," observed Freitag, "he'll behave himself, trust *me*. Mr. Bridport," she added with an embryonic sob, "knows a good woman when he meets her." He was to come, it seemed, to dinner at eight, and hoping for the best, I sank into a book as a bee sinks into a foxglove.

At seven o'clock the telephone shrieked with what somehow seemed to be no ordinary frenzy. "Damn, blast, hell," it began, "can't you get any bloody answer?" "Hello?" I said, philosophically. "Oh, that you, ole boy?" it replied. "Sorry can't be with you till nine. Those Indians. They're to be executed at 2 a.m. to-morrow Greenwich Mean Time. Executed! Can't you understand what that means? Damn it all, I thought you had a thimbleful of gumption. You're all hopeless. Look here, if those poor devils are hanged, we shall lose India. Try to get that into your thick skull. If we reprieve them, we've bound India to England for the residue of the world's history." . . . How simple, I thought, are these international, inter-racial issues, and what a pity that our clear-eyed poets are never appointed to manage them; and meanwhile the telephone vociferated, a little thickly, "Stragic! Here's opp'tunity of a lifetime, and not a soul in the Cabinet who can see beyond's nose. Running the Empire, are they? Ruining the Empire! Look here, I've been telephoning Chamberlain, Simon, Churchill, and Eden, and can't get the simplest idea into their armour-plated skulls. But those Indians——"

"Mustn't be executed," I prompted, sympathetically.

"Mushn't, mushn't," said the instrument. "If I have to stay up all ni', I'll shave them. . . ."

There was nothing for me to do but to read my book, to dine and, by remembering Bridport's poetry and his innate kindness, to prepare myself for the spirituous insults which I confidently anticipated. Sure enough, a little after nine o'clock Dicky lurched blinking into the main room. Without a pause, except for a glance at the various bottles on the sideboard, he began to tell me about two Indian agitators, how if they were executed the British Empire would immediately disintegrate, how idiotic everybody was, and I perhaps the most unintelligent of all Britons, and how Dick Bridport was determined, at any cost and single-handed, to hold the Empire together. At the first break in his wild babble I said, "Dick, you'd better have some food. It's ready, upstairs. And then what about forty winks?"

"Only a mouthful," he said, "and something to drink. Haven't had a drink since ten o'clock this morning. And by Jove, yes, I will take a nap. Half an hour, that's all. Wake me up in half an hour. Those chaps are to be murdered at 2 a.m. Greenwich Mean Time, and I'm going to keep a vigil."

Not wishing to hear the drunken gramophone of that revolving mind record again and again its exasperated conviction that everybody else in the British Empire was incredibly and incurably obtuse, I left the poet to sup alone in the room upstairs. I waited, my eyes reading a book, my attention listening alertly. To my surprise no stumbling sound came from the dining-room. I tiptoed into the passage. I told Mrs. Freitag to investigate. She returned, saying, " 'E's drunk 'is supper, and what's more he's managed to undress. 'E's in bed." Perhaps, after all, I reflected thankfully, he won't be able to keep that vigil; and then, still listening apprehensively, I went back to my book, and although more than an hour crept past I heard nothing but the nocturnal rumble of Regent Street and the noise of home-going footsteps in Savile Row. At midnight I judged the position to be safe, and stealthily went to bed.

Early the next morning, relieved that the night had passed so quietly, I donned a dressing-gown and went into the living-room.

On my desk were some sheets of paper scribbled over in faint red pencil. Verses—verses in one of those hurdy-gurdy metres which come spontaneously to a befuddled mind—but verses, all the same, filled with compassion for the two foolish Indian fanatics. "Where is he?" I said to Mrs. Freitag. Her underlip expressed anger, disillusion, and deep sympathy with herself. "Never again," she ejaculated, "abusing my hospitality, that's what I call it, and if he must drink, it won't be here! Been out, he has, trampling the streets. Four in the morning, he says. Left the door open."

I glanced at the sideboard. There was no drop left of the sherry, the benedictine, the vodka, the gin, or the Grand Marnier. They had achieved their destiny as one mighty cocktail consumed at four in the morning by the inspired poet.

"I don't trust him," Mrs. Freitag was growling, "not as I now trusts nobody. 'E can say what 'e likes, but *I* never broke it, never."

"Broke what?"

"That there little china basket what Miss Villiers give you. In smithereens, it is."

"But," I protested, "it was nowhere near his bed. It was right at the other end of the room. . . ."

A few minutes later, Dick Bridport joined me. He was surprisingly cheerful and seemed no longer to be at all apprehensive about the Empire. "Sorry," he said, "about that china basket. I always wave my arms about, you know, when I'm asleep." I was glad that he had forgotten the two agitators. He tossed his cigarette-end into the electric fire.

V

BURIED TREASURE

MEN who are highly fastidious about wine and food may be uncomfortable friends, and on the whole I prefer the good fellow who can make merry over a tin of sardines. The

3

experts, moreover, can be really tiresome as when a famous claretist had promised to dine with me. In order that he might be happy I walked to Pall Mall, had a subtle consultation with an ancient firm of wine-importers, and brought back a bottle of claret which at least was worth its weight in silver. And then, just as the parlourmaid was tilting the decanter, my guest said, "No, no! Thank you! I am not allowed anything nowadays."

E. V. Lucas, too, was a man who doted on fine cookery. If I dined with him I became bored with the process of eating when there was still half a dinner to come; and if he dined with me I always wondered if he was nobly enduring a dinner which in my judgment did credit to the cook. Of course I would risk his mute anguish for the sake of enjoying his humorous and reminiscent talk, and on one occasion I invited J. C. Snaith to join us. When three cricket-lovers dine together on a winter's evening, the main topic of conversation is predestined; and I remember saying to my guests, "A golfer can tell you what his handicap is, and I've just thought of a way in which we could assess a man's cricket skill. Take batting. Our friend Charles Fry could certainly not remember how many hundreds he had scored, and neither could Mr. Hobbs. They would have to consult Wisden. Now, you," I said, glancing at the lean and melancholic Snaith, "could tell us the tally of your centuries, but you could not say how many times you have made over eighty. You are, therefore, an eighty-man, just as I am a mere forty-man. . . ."

"You could apply your method," commented E. V., "to bowlers. You'd say 'Spiffkins, how often have you taken eight or nine or all ten wickets?' Of course, not every bowler is named George Washington. . . ."

"No," said Snaith, who was so soon to die of diabetes, "our host's idea is ingenious but fallacious." He turned to me. "My son," he observed, "so much depends on the class of cricket which you are accustomed to play." But I countered this by suggesting that first-class bowlers operating at the Oval are not more formidable than the blacksmith on a cow-cropped wicket.

I had guessed that Snaith was a dying man, and I had wanted to see him again. I knew also that he and Lucas were old friends: they had played, I believe, for J. M. Barrie's cricket team. I was now, perhaps, fifty, or very close upon it; and I had known Snaith since I was twenty-two. In the passing of those twenty-eight years I had seen the steady decline of his reputation as a novelist. It was, I think, in 1901 that, coming from the drab and uninspiring town of Nottingham, he achieved considerable success with his Meredithian novel, *Broke of Covenden*; and when he composed that notable work he was, I believe, not more than twenty-two or three. But he lived in a dream, like the "dumb" hero of his queer story, *William Jordan, Junior* (acclaimed by AE as a rare specimen of mysticism in an Englishman); and although he lost admiration decade by decade, I do not think that he ever saw himself as a mere hack-novelist, or perceived that his literary career had been a long diminuendo.

When I heard of his death, my imagination replayed a number of cricket matches in which "J. C." had figured as my most accomplished player: he had indeed played three or four times for Notts County, and that in itself is a form of the *Légion d'honneur*, a neat little red ribbon in the buttonhole of a mere novelist. I thought again of *Broke*, *The Sailor*, *William Jordan*, *Araminta* (partly written in my lovely old Wiltshire manor-house), and I felt that the hurrying world, with its absurd preference for what is newest, would perhaps never open those books again: and because I had loved my stoical old friend, and had known him when I was in the sapful twenties, and now wondered if the new men (all of whom, it seemed, actually had "genius") were really better craftsmen and better life-lookers than that tall, emaciated, generous-hearted, humble and humorous author who, as we say, had failed.

And then, as that evening lengthened I began to muse upon the absurdity of fashions in literature. I thought of the "slim volumes"—poetry, of course—which a world preoccupied by Shaw, Wells, or Noel Coward had allowed to sink into the ooze of oblivion. But who was I to talk about the ooze of oblivion? The very poets whom I had in mind, whose works

I looked forward to reconsidering, might be fancying that mankind still read their verses, might not at all appreciate my deep-sea diving for their sunken treasure. . . . Still, there were those little books on the shelves of my Sheraton bookcase, and I settled down, by the electric fire, to have a good evening with them.

Real poetry is not subject to fashion. Only foolish reviewers conceive, for example, that a verse-book which has been composed under the influences of nineteen-forty is likely to be of more interest or higher value than a verse-book which came out of the influences of nineteen-hundred. If either book contains any true poetry—even a few lines—that part of it will not be affected by the changes of forty years: but there is always, and there is now, a large amount of verse which is as much a product of its period as the slang of any particular decade. Nearly all the verse in *The Yellow Book* has become so seriously weathered as no longer to be worth tasting, and it is obvious that imitations of Mr. T. S. Eliot will not live longer than imitations of Lord Tennyson. First of all, then, I pick up a book which appeared in 1908, and I find that most of the poems in it are diffuse and lack precision, but I find also true emotion. The poet hears a lark singing in the afternoon—

> Its liquid flood of mirth
> As rare a boon
> To thirsty ears as God's dew is to earth.

Now, "mirth" is a mere piece of putty, a rhyme-born word, and we ought not to pass it without wincing, nor do I feel that there was any need to drag in God. The dew by itself is all that the poem needs. Moreover, the poet goes on to say:

> Yet it is afternoon.
> I thought the larks, all scorning
> The jaded hours, sang only in the morning.

and again we have to put a bad mark against that unnecessary word "all," in the second line. But then the poet, coming to what she had first wanted to say, writes admirably. Listen!

> And I, whose first flushed youth is going,
> Who watch the swift noon growing

> Upon me, hour by hour,
> Feeling that I must always stand apart
> From earth's sweet singers, because I lacked the pow'r
> To loose the morning song-burst from my heart—
> Oh, songster of the mellowing hour of day,
> Shall I, too, late or soon,
> Learn from your throat the way
> To loose my power of song even in my afternoon?

Yes, I mused, that's good, that's alive still, and would it not be well if we recognised that poetry is indeed "the morning sun-burst from the heart" and that, in consequence, hardly any man can achieve poetry after the age of forty. . . . At forty a man should prepare to give up verse-writing as he prepares to give up squash-rackets or lawn-tennis.

I had on my shelves another and more recent book by the same writer. Indeed, it was published ten years later. Here again I found jewels: but I knew that those who are afraid of emotion would despise what I was admiring. Again, I have always felt that if women are to write novels and poems they should write like women, should lead from strength, should contribute to literature something which even the most imaginative of men could not do so well. So of course I was pleased with two markedly feminine poems which, nevertheless, had been hall-marked by that artistry without which an emotional writer may merely be spilling words like water.

> Farewell, you children that I might have borne.
> Now must I put you from me year by year,
> And year by year the root of life be torn
> Out of this womb to which you were so dear;
>
> Now year by year the milky springs be dried
> Within the sealed-up fountains of my breast,
> Now year by year be to my arms denied
> The burden they would break with and be blessed.

A man might easily apprehend vaguely that grief of the barren woman which this poem so vividly transmits, but he could not have expressed it with such effective abandon. I do not believe, either, that a man could have written *The Outlet*. A well-sexed man would be too selfish to have met with this situation: an epicene man would not have been capable of transforming it into a poem.

> Grief struck me. I so shook in heart and wit,
> I thought I must speak of it or die of it.
>
> A certain friend I had with strength to lend:
> When mine was spent I went to find my friend,
>
> Who, rising up with eyes wild for relief,
> Hung on my neck and spoke to me of grief.
>
> I raked the ashes of my burned-out strength
> And found one coal to warm her with at length.
>
> I sat with her till I was icy cold.
> At last I went away, my grief untold.

I laid aside those two verse-books by Eleanor Farjeon, reflecting, a little sadly, that she is one of the few among my friends whom I knew on the further side of two European wars; and picking out a verse-pamphlet (*Wild Geese*, by Brian Hill), I found a small poem which made me regret that there was no poetry-lover on the opposite side of my electric fire.

> Quite suddenly the crowd began
>   To waver, sway, and part,
> Till o'er the heads my eyes met yours,
>   And, O, my beating heart
>
> Became a singing bird to see
>   Your wistful searching eyes,
> And all the beauty of your face
>   Light with a glad surprise.

How surprising, I said to myself, that anyone in 1923 could write verse with that simplicity and all that shameless emotion. But is there anybody who does not recognise the poet's experience? And has it not been sensitively recorded? Then I thought, "No! They wouldn't like it: but the truth is that clever men and epigrammatic women ought not to discourse upon poetry because no good poetry is clever. On the contrary, in the large, the healthy, the poetic eras men make their richest friendships by sharing an emotional experience, whether it comes from reading poetry aloud or from worshipping God in public."

I turned to another University poet—one who, since 1925, has made a name as a sardonic novelist. In 1925 (or probably a year or two earlier) Graham Greene wrote a poem which finely expresses the intermediate stage between 1910 and 1940, between Flecker's delight in feminine charm and the stern cerebralism of Auden, Spender, and the other bright luminaries of the moment. If we look carefully we may even acquire an uncommonly clear impression of the man behind the poem:

> I do not wish to leave this life before you,
> For I am shy and hate strange company;
> Am ignorant of the way to speak to God,
> Whether "Father," "Majesty," or simply "You There" . . .

(Please observe the capital T, for it adds humour to this mocking poem.)

> But if you go, I will follow quickly,
> And you shall introduce me to new friends,
> (How can you help but make friends with the male angels?)
> And when I skate on thin ice talking of Satan.
> Warn me with that little twisted frown of yours,
> And occasionally praise me with that same eye-glancing smile
> That made me happy at moments even upon Earth. . . .

(Is that, I wonder, just a shade too weary? Perhaps not in a gifted undergraduate.)

> But I will allow you a small start,
> So that you may say aside to Michael,
> (But for my sake be not too pleasant with him):
> "Do not mind his rudeness, he is shy:
> And do not be offended if he does not listen to your talk.
> He thinks too much on me.
> And do not, do not let him talk to God
> Of the superiority of Hell's constitution."

An undergraduate who could make fun of his own intellectual superiority over the rest of mankind was so uncanny as to suggest acrid possibilities.

Our latest bunch of poets avoid the sonnet, and certainly it is difficult to fashion a sonnet which does not smack either of

Shakespeare or Wordsworth. Wilde is, I think, alone in having taken Milton for his master—and with noble results: the sonnet

"Albeit nurtured in the democracy"

and the grand sonnet upon the sale of Keats's love-letters, will remain as beautiful works of art when nobody is any longer interested in the squalid sexual excitements of the poet. On this particular evening, however, taking down a prettily presented little book called *Happy Flame*, by Adrian Bury, I rediscovered with new appreciation a sonnet "On a Greek Bust":

> We will dispute no more; there is no peace
>   In creed or myth, nor in platonic thought;
>   The mighty word is worn and overwrought,
> There is no comfort in philosophies;
> What poet can explain life's purposes?
>   The riddle is unsolved; the mind, distraught,
>   Turns like a wheel and brings us back to naught.
> We only know that joy and loving cease.
>
> Look on this miracle of perfect grace,
>   This Attic girl with jonquils in her hair,
> With eyes at peace and lips in sweet suspense:
> Let her be mistress of our reverence;
>   Listen and love her; and she will declare
> God is but God, and beauty is his face.

I care little, if at all, for the weaknesses in this poem—"naught," "overwrought" (obsolete words and therefore lifeless), and "perfect," a word much too facile and imprecise, for the man had obviously had an experience which could better be phrased in verse than in prose, and something of his fine emotion remains.

By this time I was in the happy state of a numismatist who looks at his golden Greek drachma, his ducat bearing a grotesque representation of the Doge Giovanni Dandolo, and his unclipped Charles the First crown-piece; and lighting another pipeful of Bristol shag and offering myself a whisky-and-soda which did credit to my host, I next examined a small verse-book, published in 1924, and my attention was at once gripped by the line

"The flowers have stormed the woods to-day:"

and then how strange it was that our omniscient reviewers had
not become excited by these newly discovered fragments from
Sappho:

> If you've a mind to be glad unbind
> And scatter abroad your trammelled tresses;
> If you'll love me, unbare your breasts;
> If you'll kiss me, a thousand kisses!"

or this:

> Oh, you are fair, my love, and keen your kiss:
> Who shall avail to make your glories his,
> Who wed with you, my sword-like Thoralis?

Yes, much might have happened if Professor Andrade, instead
of inventing these lines, had translated them from a crumbling
manuscript found in the monastery on Mount Athos.

I knew very well that silly people would say, "But these are
all minor poets—and minor poems"; and my irritation caused
me to expostulate aloud, " Nearly all poems are minor! But is
there no room for the primrose as well as for the rose?" The
room vouchsafed no answer, and, turning to a pair of charming
little books by Cecil French, I noticed with surprise that the
earlier one was published in 1922, the later one in 1927. Here
was the handiwork of a craftsman decidedly more self-exacting
than any of my previous poets; and although I have never been
sure of what Rossetti meant by "fundamental brainwork" (as
the basis of all good art), I suspected that scrupulous artistry
—the weighing of every word in the millimetrical scales of a
goldsmith—might not be far from the meaning of that "king
of men." Here, certainly, I had found it. Here was work
cleansed of murkiness and generalities; here was the verse-craft
of a man who was able also to enrich his books with skilful
and attractive woodcuts. Did he suggest his period? Why,
yes—undoubtedly. Shannon influenced him as a draughtsman,
Yeats as a verse-man: but does it matter? Must he pine for a
communist revolution in England before we can seriously
consider his poetry? Must he write in slack verse? No, no—
here is a quite unusual personality—painter, poet, soldier, and
half-mystic, who could say of himself:

> That, wearied, I cast aside what, unwearied, I sought to find,
> Wandering unsatisfied under the wandering moon.

How packed with significance, I thought, is that first line, and how guiltlessly an "irresponsible reviewer" might read it glibly. . . . What does it say, I reflected? Does it not say that the poet when he is wearied can seek pleasure in the life of senses but, unwearied, would push onward towards a spiritual enlightenment?

I took out my magnifying lens and I scrutinised this flawless poem. . . .

> The tides pass on; gods come and go.
> Dust drowns the proudest sanctuaries,
> And long-held laws pass out of mind
> When stone from stone is fallen apart:

"But this," I exclaimed, "is of such delicate quality— reminding one of a distinguished Riesling—that I really must ring up Eric Gillett or Leon M. Lion, the only men of my acquaintance who perceive that poetry is timeless." And the poem, the poem—how did the poet complete it?

> Nothing men's hands have touched abides.
> What shall abide though worlds may cease?
> But little out of all we know—
> The fire that flickers in the wind,
> The changing of the unwearied tides,
> And the old hunger at the heart.

It is odd that the work of this fine craftsman should be quite unknown while all the reviewers in Great Britain flocked, sheep-like, to praise the *Last Poems* of A. E. Housman, a book which contains only one memorable line, and "The Testament of Beauty," which is possibly the flattest and most dreary of all printed poems since the vogue of Beattie or Dr. Blackmore. But five years later, in 1927, what has our quiet, our unacknowledged, word-artist to give us?

Alas, the man in a hurry (did I mean a reviewer?) would never stay long enough, I thought sadly, to savour the mystical emotion of two poems which now caused me to gloat like a bee. Mystical emotion is, I dare say, not common property. Perhaps we ought not to expect a reviewer to hear its peculiar overtones.

> "Exiles from we know not where" . . .

Surely, a startling line? Not startling at all, of course, if you do not put your mind to it. . . .

> Exiles from we know not where,
> Exiles driven now here, now there,
> What do we in the world to-day—
> We who hold some memory
> Of the joy that was our share
> In the world's lost yesterday . . .

Would most readers allow the rhythm and melody of these lines to float them unthinkingly along? But "the world's lost yesterday," can it mean anything but that the poet has had memories of other earth-lives? That is just what he did imply, as we shall now see, and his words will make soft nostalgic echoes in the spiritual core of any man who has tasted the same experience:

> Was it in resounding Rome,
> By some calm Hellenic shore,
> In half-fabulous lands maybe,
> Rose the erewhile heart-held home
> That we dream of evermore?

"Resounding," "calm," and "heart-held" are exquisitely judged words which the poet would not have found unless he had dived deep and searched long. And how does he end this lovely reverie?

> Now, nor south, north, east, nor west
> Holds the place where we would rest
> In this iron-bound, bleak to-day.
> Exiles driven now here, now there,
> Crazed by broken memory,
> What do we in the world now, say—
> We who lived when joy was—we
> Exiles, exiled—O from where?

A goldsmith working with gold-leaf dares hardly breathe, and this poet, in my fancy, used words as though they were gold-leaf: and, filling another pipe, I thought I would examine another of his poems. He had called it "Before the Glass," and, savouring the rhythms, I read:

> The face that meets me in the indifferent glass . . .

(I paused to admire "indifferent.")

I am wearied of. Too well—or it would seem—
I know its lines and planes—all that will pass
Leaving me living as I live in dream.

Does he mean anything, or is he anticipating a subsequent style
in verse? Surely, the man means that when the sense-battering
experiences of "life" are ended, he will find himself in a state
which he now can only attain during sleep?

In dream, forsooth, I have found it otherwise;
The self, in that more fluid world more free,
May live and love under what strange disguise
Of form, of speech—yea, even of memory.

In sleep, in death—beyond the ivory gate—
What waits the pilgrim of the ephemeral?
What form of glory or shadow—form, fate, state
Of king, priest, harlot, hunted criminal?

This deep-down, exactly worded poem made no more impression upon the world, it seems, than its companion, the poem
which I had just left.

And last of all, I opened again a book called *Love Poems of
a Musician*, and was at once impressed by the line:

The endless grey sea-sorrow and murmuring miles

I was then wholly charmed by the anonymous musician's
account (in "Nympholept") of a spring day during which he
found himself in a

Woodland pied with primrose-fire

and suddenly beheld a wood-nymph or other pre-Christian
sprite

with hair
Blown wide, and amber bosom bare,—

to which Polonius might have muttered " 'amber' is good."
The poem continues in this charming style:

I stared. She stared; then sudden flung
Her brown chin up, and to the sky
Jeered with an antic mirth, whilst I
To mad-cap life was pricked and stung
By the sweet taunting of her tongue.

> I tossed aside the dismal book
> And tore to shreds my sober gear.
> Away she scampered, feigning fear,
> And—her bare shoulder for my guide—
> I chased all day the elfin bride. . . .

and in the end, I am happy to report, he captured that "birth of wanton Spring with pointed ears and slanted eyes."

But, indeed, I had hardly ceased envying the poet such a gay experience when, coming upon a grim poem about "The Battle of the Somme," I discovered a quite different aspect of this varied writer:

> God—after this unholy push
> He might get Leave—
>   aye, leave to crush
> Her white warm body up to him,
> Strained close till this bad world went dim

(I relished that line.)

> To slake his dusty lips for hours
> Upon her crimson bosom-flowers.
> The Soul? bah! let it cry for backers
> To lounging bards and fiddling slackers.
> The flesh's throb and sting of fire
> Sufficed for a live Man's desire.

I thought I had already perceived a significant difference between the poems of this musician and the poems of Cecil French, who, as I have said, was a skilled maker of woodcuts. There was a more delicate melody in the musician's verse, a finer appreciation of form and economy in the work of the artist. And sure enough, I now met with a poem devised upon such a delightful and novel metre that I insisted upon reading it aloud to myself. He begins by telling how "all that stolen day of May" he and his love-girl had blissfully idled in a boat on the river near Shiplake. They must have landed, perhaps for a picnic lunch or tea, seeing that

> Then in the sleepy meadows she slipped down among the clover,
>   And tumbled in the flowers and grass
>   Knew well how maddening-sweet she was,
> While she blew off the country-clocks and laughing told them over,
> Disdainful of their freakish tale, having the world for lover.

> But when alone at chill of dusk I heard the ripples shiver,
>   Not near so high of heart as she
>   To front the whims of destiny,
> While sedges murmured, "Sometime?" and poplars whispered, "Never?"
> Sighing I shook a doubtful head and turned home from the river.

"God bless my soul!" I exclaimed (having a taste for vigorous old-world ejaculations), "the man who is not charmed by that tune and by the sentiment of the poem and by its deft indication of two temperaments, does not deserve to have learned the alphabet." And again lighting my pipe, I reflected upon the aesthetic and emotional pleasure which these many unknown poems had given to me; and for a moment I caught sight of all the verse which has ever been written, and wondered if it was was like the burgeoning and annual reburgeoning of some ancient apple-tree which, though for the most part prone on the grass, vigorously refuses to die, so that if the leaves of a year or the verses of a generation enjoy their life for a little while and are then forgotten, we ought not to be surprised and we ought not to lament. Nature is a very Branwell Bronte for wastefulness, and so is the Muse of Poetry. Nature, indeed, has so little in common with the frugal French and so much with the extravagant English that any professor could easily explain the preoccupation of our own poets with trees and mountains rather than with buildings and personalities.

Would Time dry up the juice which I had found in these poems? Would they fail to charm the men of a hundred years hence? If students continue to peruse the Greek Anthology, though much of it is withered wood; and the works of Symmachus and Ausonius, who strove heroically to sustain Latin literature when the Roman world was doomed; and even the verses of Stephen Duck or Alexander Smith (neither of whom, I had to admit, was quite negligible), why, in the name of my own distracted period, should not these poems, which had made my evening so memorable, continue to find responsive readers?

Then, prone—as every human being is prone—to self-pity, I reflected upon all the noble and lovely and eye-amazing poems which will be written, or dictaphoned, by unborn poets, by poets who will be at their best so many years or even lustres

after I and this world have parted company: but, ever scornful
of self-pity, I cured myself by thinking of all those less fortunate
men who had been born so early that they could never read
the "Ode to a Grecian Urn," "Tears, idle tears," or "When
lilacs last in the dooryard bloomed." There had even been
miserable troglodytes who left the world before Shakespeare
had penned a line; and thinking about the beautiful poems
which Russian, American, and Icelandic poets may create when
my day shall be long since over, I suffered a faint and foolish
melancholy, and began to wonder whether my youthful
conviction of metempsychosis was, after all, a genuine divina-
tion.

But poetry in the future will, I imagine, be less diffuse. Dante
and perhaps Carducci are the only European poets who never
permitted their work to sprawl. Our mental kinship with the
old Greeks ought to have made "The Faerie Queene," "The
Prelude," "The Excursion," together with most of Browning's
verse and most of Swinburne's unperpetrateable: and now that
we have some knowledge of the Chinese poet's economy, we
may hope that our own poets will write with more care and
less volubility.

VI

A DESPERATE SOUL

I MIGHT have understood her behaviour—might, indeed,
have understood what really happened between them—if I
had known her better; but she and I were the merest acquain-
tances. It is no exaggeration and no conventional phrase to
say that in everybody's opinion Veronica Lulworth was one
of the most beautiful young women in London. Old Thomas
Middleton might well have had her in mind when he wrote:

> 'tis a spark of beauty
> Able to set a world at gaze,

and what is more, she was, so far as I could make out, full of kindness and goodwill towards both men and women even if, as I remember thinking, she could not quite be called "warm-hearted." Her affectionate manner was like sunlight, universal but impersonal. She had some taste for all the arts—music in particular—but nobody would have claimed that she was well-read. In fact, one of her best friends—also an actress—remarked to me once, "Vere's much too busy enjoying the world to be much of a reader. D'you know, I can't remember to have seen her with a book. Oh, yes—once: and then it was an American book called *The Body Beautiful*."

I knew Geoffrey very much better; and, in common with everybody else who was acquainted with both of them, I was astonished when it became evident that he had not only fallen deeply in love with Veronica, but was actually in pitiful anguish. At the time he was certainly not less than forty-five, and he had come through a considerable number of attachments. They were always romantic and always founded upon affection with the result that all the women with whom Geoffrey had shared this or that section of his life continued to look upon him as the best of their lovers and as, afterwards, the best of their friends. But—and the point is of some interest as a clue—he told me that although he had loved seriously and even been

Eaten by jealousy to the inmost bone,

he thought he had never quite lost his head or his heart. "I always knew," he said, "that at a pinch I could manage without her. It must be terrifying if you're utterly obsessed by a dire need of someone's personality—as Hazlitt was when he fell in love with that silly servant girl." It is true that Veronica was no servant girl and not silly and not vicious, but within a year or two of his saying those words, Geoffrey—to his own astonishment—was a victim of that "love-madness" to which Plato refers. And in view of his lifelong passion for literature, as indeed of his own fine literary achievement, we onlookers were completely mystified by Destiny's choice of Veronica. She would have been quite at sea in the small London world which cares passionately for the art of writing, and would not have understood a word of those long flights into mystical philosophy in which he surpassed any man of my experience. What is the cause, we wondered? Just her supreme beauty? But he had known her for years and had not cared much about her. Why had she suddenly obsessed him? And what did he truly want? Surely not marriage? Why, she is so altogether unsuitable that in a few months he would be in a state of continual exasperation. And why, if she did not want him as a lover, must she go about with him almost everywhere? She might, we admitted, be merely a sex-teaser, but, as I have said, she was temperamentally kind and it was therefore incomprehensible that she could watch him suffering so acutely and yet remain happy herself. Yes, we used to wonder how it had all begun. I knew how it had ended, for Geoffrey, dropping in at Albany one day a little before Christmas, told me that he had booked a berth on a liner which was going to West Africa, "because," he said, "for a sickness of the soul there is no cure like the sea." When he returned from that trip, he was better and calmer; and Veronica had hastily married. One evening he gave me a small sealed packet. "A sort of diary," he explained; "make any use of it you like when I've 'gone far away into the silent land.'"

It was on another winter's evening that I opened the packet. It contained a thin octavo notebook and was about half-filled. At first I found only stray sentences (some of them witty and some wise), outlines of stories, the framework of two or three plays, and a number of poems—evidently in the experimental stage: but, turning the book the other way up, I came upon the "sort of diary." He had scribbled it on board the liner, and as I read it the whole story gradually developed as though it were a photographic negative in a chemical solution.

"December 19th.

"Away from Southampton. I had not realised how long it is since I was on a liner: twenty-three years. . . . It's dark now, and I'm writing this in a corner of the smoking-room. Thank God for whisky and tobacco.

"I am taking this voyage by an effort of will and in hope of curing a catastrophic love. Years hence the voyage will assuredly be as vague as the dream of four or five nights ago: and will my wretchedness of spirit have become equally dream-like? I am no love-sick lad, not even in the tempestuous thirties, and—having loved many times—I know that, if I do not end my life, she will some day torture me no longer. My long pain of loving, of desiring, of wanting to make her career into a masterpiece, will gradually fade. It must, inevitably it must, if only I have will enough not to step back into the circle of that ruinous enchantment.

"Between the June of 1933 and yesterday I did for her all that I possibly could, and I cared far, far too much ever to 'laugh at it.' Why did she not love me? What was wrong? She was certainly more than fond of me. 'You are the best friend I ever had,' she said. She even said, 'I don't know what I'll do if you go away for a long while.' And yet when I rushed from that doctor's dinner-party, within five minutes of the coffee being served (what on earth must the doctor's wife have thought of me?), and told her that I couldn't stand the strain any longer and had bought my berth in this ship, how instantly she rearranged her attitude. 'He's really going,' she thought (I could hear her thoughts quite plainly), 'so that curious, rather charming episode is over. I'm a little bit sorry, but, anyway, I must look out for new interests, that's all.'

"And last night, too, she did come in—for five minutes—'to wish you good-luck!' Hasn't she the faintest notion of what I have endured these twenty months? 'I expect I'll go gay,' she said, 'for about two days, and then look about for stage-work.' She 'went gay' that evening—a dinner at Quaglino's and a musical comedy. I wonder—with whom?

"December 20th.
"It is over. Of course it is—for always. In the end she will give herself to some other man, I suppose—or can she have been born without natural desire? He will not love her beauty more delicately, more intensely, than I would have loved it.
"O time, time—come to my aid! But your medicine is too slow.

"December 21st.

"I looked through my engagement-book. Why did she come so often? What did she get out of it? How restless I was on the days when I did not see her, how starvingly I waited for our next meeting, how eagerly I kept on looking out of the window if her taxi-cab was due, and what a draught of nectar was the sight of her, tall and graceful and exquisitely groomed, as she paid the cabman, and I knowing that after one more minute all that living beauty would be entering my room. Really, the number of our meetings was quite fantastic. Why did she come so often? A list of the last three months. . . .

"October 7th. Dinner at 8.15.
   8th. Lunch at the Ivy.
   10th. To see a film.
   11th. 'For ten minutes.'
   13th. She blew in with Madeleine. We dined at Jules.
   18th. Jules. I presented H. famous German producer, to her. (An attempt to break the enchantment.)
   27th. 2.15–3 p.m.
   29th. To a play.

"November 1st. 4.40–5.10.
   2nd. 7.30, for dinner here.
   4th. To Scott's for lunch.
   7th. She came at 10.40 p.m., after a rehearsal.
   10th. A theatrical midnight-party.
   13th. Farewell at my flat.
     (Another attempt not to see her.)
   19th. Jules. Lunch V., Madeleine, and Robert.
   22nd. Rushed to her (after the Doctor's dinner-party).
   25th. Lunch after a rehearsal.

"December 7th. She broke an appointment.
   10th. She dined here. Went back with her. Said good-bye.

"December 22nd.

"A great deal of this long-drawn unhappiness came, I believe, from her inability to say clearly what she felt or wished. Sometimes, too, she used phrases which meant one thing to her and another thing to me and the rest of the world. Even now I am not certain why it went wrong—after such a rare and lovely beginning. Perhaps that sonnet came somewhere near to the truth. . . .

NARCISSA

There was no mystery when I did so, too—
    For all men thrill to your fair form and face,
And in a thousand ways adore in you
    An incarnation of all human grace.
I loved you? Yes—how could I be so blind
    As not to love perfection? God forbid!
But it was terrible and most strange to find
    How fiercely I could hate you, as I did.

Then, lost, quite lost, I recognised too late
    That rival whom before I could not see,
Whose beauty is, like music, so intense
That the soul drowns within the wavering sense.
What wonder if I sometimes flashed with hate,
    Since we both loved one woman, and you she!

"I sent it to her, supposing that she'd glance at it, not understand it, and leave it lying about: but when she next came to see me, she said, 'I'm rather proud of that poem, darling, but don't write any more, will you? I don't want to be burned alive.' I do suspect narcissism. Her frank, affectionate, highly misleading manner has given her the wildest reputation for 'promiscuity'; but in my belief she has only attempted affairs with perhaps two men, and found no happiness in either venture. Just because she is under-sexed, she has only a very dim appreciation of the effect which her ways or her unconsidered words are making upon men. Her long, large eyes are the colour of star-sapphires. Once she sent me a part of a photograph—just those two soft languishing eyes—with a note saying, 'What do you think of my new visiting-card?' And another time she said, 'Yes—somebody once called them "boudoir eyes.'" All this, which would seem mere heartless man-teasing, may in her have been an innocent, half-playful amusement and delight in possessing a beauty which caused so much disturbance. I discovered many emotions which I had either never dreamed of or had no more understood than I understand the Einstein theory. The strangest of all was a sense (it began when I'd loved her for almost a year) that she imparted her beauty to anything that she touched. Her beauty was of the ideal type—aristocratic and suggesting deep poetry —and it came to affect me as some people might be affected by the holiness of a saint. It was like some delicate and exalting emanation. It made me realise why medieval people had supposed there was magic in the laying-on of hands. It made me remember how savages believe in the *mana*, the invisible effluence, which resides in certain objects and persons. I could see quite easily why kings had been looked upon as divine. I completely understood how extreme physical beauty had really seemed unearthly and sacred to the ancient Greeks. If Veronica touched a book, the book retained for some time a fragrance from her personality. This was no pretty fancy which I had made up. It was an experience which took me by surprise, and it was so irrational that I sometimes rebelled against it.

"But there's another cause for our luckless disharmony. How on earth did I blunder along for all those months without seeing something so obvious: and to think that it was she who found the phrase for it! When I fled from the doctor's dinner-party I was determined to

> put it to the touch,
> To win or lose it all.

She was used enough to the ravings of thwarted men, but she was certainly not used to any bitterness or even reproach from me, and she looked startled and somewhat unhappy. At my most wretched I could not have been abject, not for a moment, and I dare say she was puzzled and even attracted by the pride and basic independence of a man whom she had kept at arm's length for the best part of two years. At this meeting, almost our last, I explained to her with some vehemence how completely she had misled me in those earliest days, how difficult it was to believe that she really didn't know what she was saying, and so on. And while I was unpacking my heart in words, how lovelier than ever before she looked—for she had gone to bed early, and had opened the flat-door herself a little cautiously,[1] and now we must have made a fine picture, she in a night-gown and wrap, I in the black and white uniform of one who has left a dinner-party.

"After some while she said quietly and deliberately, 'I could never be in love with an introvert.' I knew in a split second how stupid it had been of me to expect from her the sensitive insight and the subtle apprehensions of the introvert. 'You talked too much' (meaning 'you probe too much into our feelings towards each other'); 'you ought to have done things, gone with me to theatres, parties, walked with me in Richmond Park.' I was taken aback. The explanation of all that woe looked suddenly so simple. I saw how patiently she must have endured those very efforts to explore our spiritual chemistry which were, I had always assumed, of the greatest interest.

"If I had understood that I was an extreme introvert who had fallen in love with an extreme extravert, I might possibly have pulled up in time. Sometimes she would ring up before coming to dinner and would say, in her low soft voice, 'I shan't be very gay.' Once she surprised me by saying, 'No, but I think you're morbid.' Only an extravert could suppose that she must always be 'gay': and by 'morbid' she merely meant that I was always trying to extract the essential meaning of a deed or a phrase. I supposed that she meant 'over-sexed,' and the retort that she was therefore my opposite manifestly bewildered her.

"I saw that I must somehow smash this enchantment. I asked her, point-blank, that desperate question which I had never quite dared to utter lest the answer should be 'No.' It was then that she spoke of 'an introvert.' I kissed her and said good-bye, and went home along the wet and lamp-reflecting streets.

[1] In view of her marriage, three months later, she may have supposed that her late visitor was someone else. (C. B.).

"My obsession had made me physically ill. I knew that, by several symptoms, and I think I had never believed that 'love' could really make a sick man of a lover. I did not give suicide more than a flying thought, and I remember thinking at that very instant, in the taxi, that most suicides are probably extraverts, probably persons who are utterly incapable of working upon their failures and unhappiness, who are nonplussed by disaster, who, in a word, decide, as usual, to seek refuge in 'action.'

"But also I still wondered how far, if at all, she was aware, in the sunrise of my passion, that she was enticing and misleading me. If she really supposed that I was sexually indifferent to her, she must have been amazingly ignorant. I do not believe that, on the contrary, she was responsible for her handiwork. In fact, if she hadn't been so unusual and half-fey, I dare say I should have said at once, 'Oh—very well, then! I've no time to waste on a baggage.' What was it that held me?

"December 23rd.

"Madeira looks as much like Paradise as it did in the old days. God! what a place for a pair of young lovers with undimmed senses, high hopes, and a pleasant income!

"When I get back (some time in March), I must resolutely carry out a new life. I must see little of her—otherwise I might stray back into that labyrinth of frustrated emotion. I must school myself to care much less about what is happening to her. I might even write well again if my mind were not hourly a prey to longing and distress: and certainly I ought to be able to live temperately, as I used to. Odd how I once despised men who drank too much or too often!

"December 24th.

"Yes, I had grown so accustomed to consorting with subtle introverts and to listening for overtones that I had simply taken for granted that the subtler we can make ourselves the more intensely are we alive. What happens to extraverts in a time of sorrow? They cannot get to work on themselves, I suppose. They must be like children, howling helplessly: but perhaps they cannot be very profoundly hurt?

"I thought the sea and the old sunlight were helping to heal me—and they were, only that last night (for the first time) she invaded my dreams. I was with her and with a man to whom she was engaged. And all the morning, like a fragment of music, I've been mentally murmuring, 'O love, my love, had you loved but me!' What a line that is—music 'shot' with wild regret. . . .

"December 25th.

"The Sports-Chairman—a genial bookie—has discovered, though heaven knows how—that I did some boxing when I was 'up.' He knew, in fact, precisely what I *had* done, all those years ago, and the result is that I'm to referee some fights to-morrow afternoon. If somebody remembers my boxing days I'm much more delighted than by any praise of my books. There are several attractive people on board.

"December 27th.

"I must really be getting better because at last I can face the whole story, even its beautiful and desperate beginning. Until now I have not dared to set it all out in front of myself so that I may look at it clearly and diagnose the trouble.

"Well then—here goes! I'd known Veronica for about eight years, but not well. Meeting her in theatres, at parties, and just occasionally seeing her at a dinner-party in my house while I was married. At first I didn't much like her: thought she was just a pretty fool. Even her great beauty somehow made little impression on me. (Of course, I was nearly always in love with somebody else—and that may account for it!) Then she went to New York. Lived there, I think, for two years. . . . Why, yes—she said, 'I used to think those two years in New York were the happiest part of my life, but now I'd say it's the present time—with you around.' That can't have been said in cruelty? . . .

"Strange—I still shrink from remembering that confident assurance of beauty which began it all. It is just as though I had brought her some masterpiece of Etruscan earthenware which, to my amazement and horror, she had instantly smashed. God knows I'm the last man to pretend that there was no lust in my love for her. On the contrary, I've maintained a thousand times that sexual lust is one of Nature's most marvellous inventions and one of our luckiest attributes: only, if it is left in its crude state, not tempered and refined, why then any slut will serve a man's need. I despise the mere lout who is worked by raw instinct, but I despise quite as much those hypocritical pseudo-mystics who pretend to themselves that lust has no part in their sex-affairs. I wanted her lovely body, and I wanted her shimmering personality, and I wanted to make real life become poetry.

"After a long strain I had separated from my wife. In marriage the natural nymph-seeking in a man is necessarily suppressed, but I had found that marriage also imposed a much more exasperating limitation. It meant, apparently, that a man could not (with any comfort in his home-life) behave with spontaneous affection towards women or express the mildest degree of admiration or, in fact, create a friendship with any woman. Free after years of circumspect behaviour, I at once restored several derelict friendships and rapidly developed some new ones: and on a summer's day I thought of Veronica, whom I cannot have seen for a year, and asked if she would lunch with me. She answered enthusiastically—on the telephone— and after a few days she was with me.

"Life in America had immensely enhanced her native loveliness. I suppose it was a matter of super-subtle body-culture and expert grooming? At least she made me forget to greet her: and, although she seemed unconscious of that beauty as being so thoroughly used to it, I continued to think, 'But I hadn't remembered that she was half so wonderful as this.' Then, the day being sunny, we went into the Park and tried, I remember, to extract the meaning from a number of very modern poems. She seemed to me an entirely sweet-natured girl, a lover of life and responsive to affection.

"We met three or four times during the next few weeks, and I began to dream that a love-affair between us might be happy and enriching. I made a few tentative approaches, and of course we kissed, but I noticed that her kisses (or rather her submission to mine) were strangely passionless. And yet all the time she was proving to me how welcome this friendship was to her.

"August drew near, and I had arranged to go with three men on a golfing holiday in the Cotswolds. Veronica came one afternoon, and being tired she lay on the sofa. She said that she was taking her holiday at a small village on the coast of North Wales. Her sister, she thought, would be with her. And suddenly she said, 'Geoffrey, darling, why don't *you* come? That would be grand!' I looked at her, with a sort of questioning smile. She persisted that I must join her in Wales, and presently I said, my whole being aglow with beautiful hope, 'I'd love to come, naturally, but it mustn't be a platonic honeymoon! You understand that, don't you!' She didn't answer, but she looked serious and nodded her head as though she were saying 'Yes' a little shyly.

"I did not see her again before we went our ways, I to the West and she to that rock-perched village of Wales.

"December 28th.

"All the week that I was with my three friends I lived in the sure conviction that soon, soon, every day sooner, I should be starting the most poetic and most heart-satisfying love-union of my life. And when she rang up—from Wales to a small hotel in Worcester—just to make sure that I did mean to come —wasn't it natural if I went back to the others, thinking, 'Oh, she wants it all as much as I do! She does, she does!'

"It was in that exultant mood that I made the long journey, reading books which I now could not name and passing cities and notable landscapes which I can hardly have looked at. And at last there at the station was Veronica, waiting. She ran forward with the world-oblivious eagerness of a lover, and getting into a horse-drawn carriage, we went along the coast to her holiday village.

"She and her sister and a woman friend of the latter had taken a fairly large cottage. 'They have the ground floor,' explained Veronica, 'and we have the first floor. Want to see your room?' Then she took me upstairs. My room was oppo-site hers. There were only two yards of landing between them, and all seemed set for a happiness never to be forgotten.

"We went for a stroll along the rocky cliffs. The day waned, and we joined the others at supper: and what with gossip about friends or about the theatre and with looking at magazines and listening to the radio, time passed, and, saying good night to the others, we climbed to our rooms.

"Through my window I heard the world-old lamentation of the sea and also that sound of an August night when the trees seem to be stretching themselves after the long sleep of a day. And after a while there was no sound in our cottage. I supposed that the sweet, long-looked-for moment had come at last, and with almost the wonder and the rapture of early youth I stepped across the landing and went into Veronica's room. She had not gone to bed. She was sitting, in her nightdress, on the edge of the bed, and was looking by candlelight at some film weekly. I was surprised when, saying, 'Hello, Geoffrey,' she went on turning those pages; but I supposed that—now when at length our pretty friendship was to die into something more splendid—she might be a little bashful.

"An instant later she was on her feet, and she cried, 'Oh, no, no! Not that—from you. Not, darling, from you. Please! I'm so tired of it all.' I went back, astonished and angry, to my room.

"In a course of a patchy night I worked hard at my state of mind. I knew perfectly well that a normal man would go off by the earliest train: but his attitude struck me as being more suitable in a spoilt child. My pride as a man and even my vanity had been nastily gashed; and yet had I been wanting only her sexhood? That, I could see, was not true. I still cared for her beauty and for her personality. I should probably have said, more simply, 'her soul.' And that night I decided to go or to stay, whichever she seemed to want when morning came: for I realised with disgust that she might think of all men as Calibans and of me as merely another.

"It was quite clear that she wished me to stay. I remained

in that cottage, under those fantastic and unnatural conditions, for perhaps a week longer; and in spite of her outcry and its echoes within my brain, I found myself becoming fonder and fonder of that exasperating friend. The hurt was so new that I had no wish to question her as to what was wrong with our relationship. I preferred to consider it secretly. If I could have foreseen my coming wretchedness and how difficult it would be ever to tear my spirit apart from hers, I should have stopped in time and have said a friendly good-bye. But, like Malvolio, I have always thought nobly of the soul, and I could not admit that any relationship, however deformed, was beyond my achievement. I said to Veronica, 'Let's go away from here, shall we?' 'All right,' said she, 'where shall we go?' 'To Warwick,' I told her—remembering how, being taken to Warwick, as a boy of eleven, I had thought of it ever since as the old, sunny heart of England.

"We stayed there for some days, putting up in a musty, comfortable inn which cannot have altered for at least a century, and of course our bedrooms were discreetly distanced by the unromantic receptionist. Each night I would grieve over all that unpraised, unthrilled, and wasted beauty of a woman. From the inn garden—old and quiet and full of old-fashioned flowers —I could see her window, nor did I ever see it without inwardly saying, 'What have you cast away, strange girl? What have we lost, and lost for ever?' She liked that garden, and she was amused by the capacious aviary with its many little birds which stood at the far end of the lawn.

"In the end we came back to London. By that time I was enchanted beyond recovery. More and more did the image of Veronica and the full syringa-like fragrance of her personality obsess me until I could hardly crawl through a day without seeing her. As for my work, it went utterly to pieces. I should not have thought that I could possibly write such rubbish—and suppose it to be good!

"Now I am slowly returning to sanity. The people here on the ship begin to excite my imagination, and that's a good symptom. But I know now what it is to love and desire until, in a panic, you find yourself out of your depth and in the grip of a current.

"The bookie has asked me to hobnob at the American Bar. And he shall hobnob with me!"

I closed the little book, and I felt that Veronica's refusal of a sex-love such as Geoffrey had brought to her was almost tragical. But still I was not certain about Veronica's psychology. Apparently she was tired of being a target for what another woman has called "the male rush." Could she not have guessed that this man was neither crude in his sexuality nor at the mercy of it? She could not see that. Even when he had proved it, she kept him at bay. Was he right, then, in declaring that she was in love with herself? There was, I thought, some evidence. And finally, how could I reconcile her acknowledged kindliness with the fact that she never did anything (even by going away) to lessen his anguish? Did she not care, or did she not see it?

I thought I would try to solve that very secret which Geoffrey had never quite solved. I wrote to Veronica Lulworth, and she came to G2. "What was wrong," I said, "between you and Geoffrey?"

He had died, and at the sound of his name those gentle calamitous eyes filled suddenly with tears. Presently she said: "I wanted him as a friend. If I'd gone to him as a lover, it would all have been finished in a month or two. It must be like that for a man."

The truth, I conceive, is that she had outstanding beauty, that she gave every promise of being an ardent lover, that men thronged to her in their thousands, that she was in reality under-sexed, that there was indeed a liberal dash of self-adoration in her make-up, that she could not distinguish Geoffrey's love-lust from the lust of men who would never have put up with her rejection; and, above all, that somehow or other the soul in her, not by any means undetectable, had never broken its shell, so that she saw the whole of life just a little bit out of focus and, being as ignorant as a five-year-old that love can become a torment, was merely bewildered by Geoffrey's variable moods and incomprehensible behaviour.

VII
BLACKWOOD'S DISEASE

WHEN I had turned fifty, a series of small events compelled me to consider gravely whether I might have become a fossil or actually an Old Fogey. In the home of my boyhood, for example, I had assumed that Wagner's music was not only "great" music, but almost perilously exciting. Now —some thirty-five years later—in walks my daughter, sits on the long, green sofa, looking much like the tall heroine in some old Icelandic story, and replies, when I ask her why she does not care for Wagner, that "his music is like suet." So, then (I pondered, not without dismay), all that rapturous love-music, glorifying life as the springtime glorifies it or striving by sheer intensity of emotion to outsoar life itself and achieve utter ecstasy in death, has become—suet! I dared not betray the shock which this word had given me, and so, chatting of politics or some other ephemeral subject, I conducted the blonde amazon upstairs to dinner.

It was not many weeks afterwards that, as an onlooker and not as a player, I joined my old cricket team at Bath, all the more pleased to do so because Peters had persuaded the young poet, Cecil Day Lewis, to join the party. I knew three or four of his poems though I had studied them through a veil of difficulty; and no doubt as a native in the Island of Poetry (for I had lived there before he was born) I must have approached him as the eighteenth-century Tahitians approached Captain Cook. A queer and intimidating figure from an unknown continent had come to disturb my happy and long-established ways: but Captain Cook sailed more than once to the South Seas, and this young poet was, in due time, to emulate the Captain and to fire his musket into the air so that I might appreciate my savage ignorance. Meanwhile at a Verse-Speaking Festival in Oxford an even better-known new poet whose name was Auden had joined the panel of adjudicators on which I too was serving. And this Auden, far from openly despising his hoary colleagues, impressed me so well that, the moment I was at liberty, off I hurried to Blackwell's—the gallant, the indispensable Blackwell—and bought one of Auden's latest books and carried it to my lodging, and settled down to an interesting and perhaps an ever-notable evening. At first I could not make any sense out of any poem in the book, but, persevering because it was obvious that Auden would not bother to write words which had no meaning, I thought I discerned that most of the poems were saying in an extremely elliptical manner (as when the Atlantic persists in surging across a speech from Washington to England) that the old social order was doomed and that a new generation was preparing to caper above its grave, fluttering a little red flag. I was discouraged and disappointed: discouraged because it had been so difficult to extract even so much meaning out of Auden's poems; disappointed because, after all my effort, he seemed not to have said anything except that the Younger Generation was Knocking at the Door. This had been stated in Norway before even my time.

Then the typhoon of another world war rushed forward, coming closer and closer, until on September the 2nd 1939 it was roaring all round us, and the lights of London were subdued to a futile glimmer. Eric Gillett, however, had previously arranged an attractive dinner-party in his book-lined flat in Earl's Court Square. Ommaney, a writer who seemed usually to be gutting whales in remote and icy waters, was to be present, and so was that admirable scholar—Cecil Day Lewis. My failure to like Auden's poems had inspired a certain terror within me, such as any of us would feel if he feared that creeping insanity had him in thrall; but Day Lewis, though he had dismissed my own archaic poetry as of no significance, had always acted and spoken benignly, and so, hoping that he would continue to suffer Old Fogies gladly, I donned evening-dress for the last time until we had peace again, or possibly for all time. Death, I knew, might remove me from my evening-suit.

I went down the monastic stone stairs of G-block and out into the Rope Walk. The lanterns under its long, old-gabled

roof were now filled with minatory dim blue bulbs. I walked
down the worn steps at the main entrance of Albany, and in
front of me lay a darkened Piccadilly. A few people went
hurriedly past me, talking with a soft intensity. London was
already awaiting the unprecedented experience of a savage
bombardment.

II

As I travelled to Gillett's flat I determined to talk at his
dinner-party as little as possible about the war and its immense
probabilities. In the first place, everyone for some weeks past
had already said everything that he had to say; in the second,
I knew well enough that no judgments or guesses or prognosti-
cations of mine could make the minutest difference to the vast
events which humanity was approaching. It seemed best, on
the contrary, to sustain interest in aspects of life which had
existed before this world-brainstorm and which were likely
some day to creep back into attention as the green art of Nature
soon reasserts itself in a ruined city or over an idle battlefield.

There would be no pertinence in recording most of our
conversation because at the moment I am merely trying to trace
the gathering alarm with which I detected symptoms of my
own fogeydom. In consequence, I will say only that, shame-
fully remembering how Auden had nonplussed me, I asked
Day Lewis, humbly but with a stiff upper-lip, why he and his
friends wrote poems which were either exceedingly difficult or
wholly impossible to understand. "Does it matter whether one
understands a poem or not?" he answered, patiently. I reeled
and invited some larger illumination. "The only question is,"
he told me, "does a poem *do* something to you? Is it an experience?" "Without meaning anything?" I queried, like a
punch-drunken prize-fighter. "Has it been an experience, that's
all that matters," he replied: and it was two or three days before
I emerged from the mental mist which immediately enveloped
me. I went home profoundly despondent about myself. I
remembered how Blackwood's Magazine, a hundred and twenty
years earlier, had made itself immortally foolish by failing to
recognise the genius of John Keats. And now it was almost

certain that I myself had contracted Blackwood's Disease! Was
not the salient symptom an inability in the sufferer to digest
any new forms of art which may appear when he has passed
the age of forty: and I was yet older, yet older. . . . Conceive
my desolation.

III

Europe was in convulsions, and Poland was being flayed
alive. It was hard not to let this knowledge obsess and disrupt
our minds: but it is useless to wring your hands where you can
give no help, and if your newspaper tells you that an earthquake
has killed ten thousand persons at some place which is half a
million miles away, you merely waste your emotional resources
if you lament without being able to assist. Indeed, you will do
better by the world if you do not add to its current unhappiness.

That is why, having gone back to the work which then lay
upon my table, I continued to think about Blackwood's Disease:
and all of a sudden I remembered how in 1918, as a censor of
the news, I had worked under and opposite a charming old
cavalry officer, a Colonel Wright. . . . Yes, and there was a
June evening when the Press Bureau telephone rang, and the
attendant said that the call was for me. I heard my sister
speaking. After she had rung off, I went to the Colonel, who
was busy with telegrams for the newspapers, and I said,
"Colonel, my father is dying, and they would be glad if I could
be there. May I go?" "My dear boy," said the old cavalry
officer, not without emotion, "of course, of course. God bless
you!" And with that, he got up and gripped my hand. Twenty
years later he would, I suppose, have been classified by our
intellectuals as a Blimp. . . . But the relevance of old Colonel
Wright to my present haunting fear is that he loved poetry
but had not progressed beyond Pope and Dryden. In a vain
attempt to educate him I lent the Colonel *A Shropshire Lad*,
and after two days he put it back into my hand, saying, "No,
no . . . it has no music." Housman—no music? Auden—no
meaning? The nightmare parallel between Colonel Wright and
myself—in 1918 and in 1939—left me in a state of extreme
consternation.

5

Worse was to come. Only a week afterwards I incautiously read a clear and fascinating article about Modern Art.[1] The writer outlined the progress of painting. He maintained persuasively that most changes in the art of painting have been wholesome or even inevitable developemnts. Giotto's naïvety had to give way before the idealistic but representational style of Leonardo. The camera had contributed much to the fine detail of Frith's "Derby Day." The impressionists were interested, he told me, in "the *wind* in the trees, rather than the trees themselves . . ., the *vibration* of sunlight, the *atmosphere* (physical or psychic, I wondered?) of the café and the law court," and so on. The cubists, I learned, had striven to concentrate upon the concealed geometrical substructure of visible objects—seeking, possibly, for the German Ding-an-sich: and in the wild fantasies of the Surrealists my guide detected the influence of Freud's doctrine of the subconscious. I was hoping for some light upon Constructivism and other yet later movements, when I came upon a sentence at the end of which I could see a faint glimmer of hope. "In course of time," said my guide, "this question of structure became more and more absorbing, until at last the geometric basis of things came to be regarded as more interesting and more important than the things themselves, so that by a gradual process of elimination their appearance was merged into a visual but abstract harmony of lines and planes intersecting and repeating one another in patterns of endless variety, *that are more akin to the involutions and evolutions of certain musical forms than to anything else.*"

As I studied this passage I could not help feeling that men —and artists—must be in a poor state of health if they can be more interested in "the geometric basis of things" than in "the things themselves"; but the important words, uttered so casually, were "musical forms." I remembered the kindliness with which Day Lewis had done his best to show me that I lost nothing if I did not understand what I was reading, and that a poem had only to make a general effect or, as he put it, to give the reader an experience. But I thought I could now see that, according to my preceptors, both poetry and painting

[1] By E. H. Ramsden.

(or drawing, or incising a sheet of cardboard) were attempts
to make upon the reader or the percipient an effect somewhat
comparable with that of music. Now, music (I said to myself)
is indeed the strangest, perhaps the loveliest, and perhaps the
most powerful, of all human arts; but it has one shortcoming
—that it lacks the emotional precision of language and those
definite associations with human life which are (or used to be)
characteristic of painting. No composer can be sure that he
has made every listener muse upon "the happy autumn fields"
and not upon some other subject of gentle melancholy; nor
can he exalt the loveliness of a woman or record the grandeur
of a landscape with the unmistakability of Titian or Turner.
Is it not foolish, therefore, to set up poetry and painting in
competition with music while, at the same time, denying to
them that very definition of meaning in which music must for
ever be entirely out of the running?

That seemed to me clear enough—self-obvious, in short: but
I knew that the world would pay no attention to common sense
and would greatly prefer to go on following its fashions into
a stagnant backwater.

IV

I began to feel hopeful about my condition, but it is foolish
to assume too easily that our seeming symptoms have no significance. And so when, a few days afterwards, Desmond Hawkins,
looking uncannily like Rameses the Second, came to see me,
I said, "Now, Desmond—pray, tell me, do not your modern
poets derive ultimately from Manley Hopkins? Is he not the
miraculous Victorian, the Stone-Age Auden, who managed to
write evocative nonsense even in the eighteen-eighties?"

And then to my amazement Desmond replied, "No. I think
Hopkins is a minor and subsequent influence. The new poetry
comes from the Pound-Eliot-Hume group as it existed in—
was it?—1910." While he spoke these words, a great burden
dropped from my back. I was almost certain that I did not
suffer from "Blackwood's"—for just as doctors refer to
"Bright's," so do they mutter (behind their hands) "Blackwood's."

I had met T. S. Eliot once and Ezra Pound half a dozen times. Hume, who was killed in the Four Years War, had at least fought a friend of mine in Café Royal. And the year 1910 did not seem to me remote—I could not class it with the days of Ashur-banipal or Rameses. I remembered it even minutely.

For me—threatened with "Blackwood's"—the point was that in 1910, a year in which I was indisputably young, I had thought of Hume's versicles as pretentious trifles, and had felt that there was in Pound's bluster more smoke than flame. But already in 1910, I was refusing to be drum-beaten into admiration of Wells and Bennett and even Bernard Shaw. Could there have been something wrong with me? Or could there have been something wrong with "the world"? Now, if I could find no nourishment in the poetry which bubbled fresh from the cow in 1939, and if I had found no joy in the prolix works of Shaw and Wells in 1910, it looked very much as though I were not only an Old Fogey, but must have been a Young Fogey, too, and possibly even a Born Fogey. That was a horrifying picture. I could see myself, in the cradle, a wizened and predestined Fogey, hearing the guns of Queen Victoria's first Jubilee, and struggling toothlessly to make out that poetry had perished with the death of the late Lord Byron.

All new movements, all attempts to break new ground, are obstructed by the middle-aged and the old; that is the perennial declaration of the young: and when we ourselves are young and revolutionary, the list of life-breathing artists who have met with senile opposition appears to recede into the dimmest windings of the past. We think triumphantly of Epstein, Beardsley, Gauguin, Manet, Wagner, Bizet, the Pre-Raphaelites, Shelley, Keats, and Mozart, and we assume that the list could be indefinitely prolonged.

The assumption, I thought, might be worth examining, and I instantly detected two large flaws in it. The first is that "new movements" are not now remembered if they were unsound and therefore did not succeed. Thus, for example, what shall we say of "the Spasmodics"? They were a group of English poets who flourished in the eighteen-fifties and whose last faint representative is Alexander Smith. Now, Smith was acclaimed in his youth as a poet superior to Tennyson and to Keats.[1] If an old reader, taking up Smith's "Poems" in 1852, had said that the verses were sham stuff and appealed only to a passing taste, would not Smith's contemporaries have pitied the old fogey, and yet would he not have been right? Again, if anyone remembers the name of Robert Montgomery, he does so only because Macaulay took the trouble to annihilate an absurd reputation. Suppose a later Macaulay were to smash the glassy reputation of . . ., but I refrained from blasphemous thoughts, and fell to considering the melancholy fate of the Della Cruscans, once a band of innovators who might comfortably have jeered at their critical elders. Indeed, my imagination went right back to the cultivated Romans of A.D. 400, and I recalled how the poet Symmachus had written a letter to his friend the poet Ausonius, a letter in which "while he gently ridicules the minute description of the fishes of that river"—the Moselle, about which Ausonius had written a poem—"yet he has no hesitation in ranking his friend with Virgil." The poet, we learn, not without benefit, "returned the compliment by attributing to the oratory of Symmachus all the force and graces of the oratory of Isocrates, Demosthenes, and Cicero."[2]

I could not doubt for an instant that Ausonius and Symmachus, poor hopeful shades, had been wholly sincere in their estimates of one another's achievement, but I did seem to discern, by this time, that there can be new and heady "movements" which die away in the desert sand.

Another consideration almost rid me of my fears. It was not merely that all artists, like clever children, are crying out "Look at me, look at me!", nor was it that any Undergraduate, conscious of his pulsing personality, will strive to express it either by fantastic verse or fantastic haberdashery; but rather that I perceived, on consideration, how few great artists have, in fact, violently departed from the norm of their age, and how

---

[1] A contemporary news-sheet said, "Let the praise sound extravagant as it may, Alexander Smith is a finer poet than Keats, in the very qualities in which Keats was finest." Tennyson wrote a letter of appreciation to Smith who, ostentatiously, used the letter as a pipe-spill. Suppose Hardy had written to . . .

[2] *Roman Society in the Last Century of the Western Empire.* Samuel Dill.

innovators—far from being obstructed—were, until recent times, enthusiastically acclaimed by young and old alike. In 1895, when *A Shropshire Lad* appeared, was Housman a traditionalist or a revolutionary? He was neither. On the one hand, he was not imitating Wilde or the other fashionables of the time; on the other, he observed strict rhyme and metre, like any Tennysonian. His originality was not startling because it was unconscious and innate, like personal charm; and he may no more have known that his verse had a new sound in it than he knew what his voice was like when heard by alien ears.

Patmore, Matthew Arnold, and Rossetti did not tear themselves out of English literary development with the violence of the Moon when she wrenched herself out of the Pacific Ocean: and yet those three poets are so distinctive that we can recognise their handiwork without the help of their signatures, and they were distinctive because they could not be anything else. That is the point, and it is a point which gave me some comfort. Perhaps, after all, I was not suffering from "Blackwood's." . . .

Or, musing upon old painters, what did I find? There are notable differences between Fra Angelico, Botticelli, Leonardo, Michelangelo, Rubens, and Holbein, but—so I said to myself, as Amaryllis handed to me the evening letters—every one of these painters would have found much to like and admire in the work of all the others. Why was it, therefore, that I, who prefer liking to disliking, could not find any pleasure in the tormented English of Auden and Dylan Thomas? I could have understood my incapacity if in my own young years I had lustily followed the fashions; had made one in that exuberant chorus which, in the first decade of this century, saluted the work of Shaw, Bennett, and Wells; if, growing older, I had stopped there, unable to stay the course any longer: if, in a word, I had dropped out, panting: but I had never cared for Shaw, Bennett, or Wells, never cared for Pound or Eliot, never responded even to the Impressionists who, God knows, were by this time almost archaic. It seemed, therefore, that perhaps there are two kinds of artist—those who by temperament paddle along the main stream and those who, at the risk of ending up in backwaters, principally desire to get away from the main stream and, in consequence, paddle themselves down any unmapped creek.

Those who keep to the main stream may merely be imitators of their elders. For a time they can win a considerable reputation. In their own day both Edwin Arnold and Lewis Morris, a couple of milk-and-water Tennysonians, must have lived in the delusion that they were poets of importance. The backwater poets, puny Ajaxes defying the lightning, may fret and strut their hour upon the stage, and for some years they can dominate their earnest coteries, but the world may see, in the end, that they were like so many children walking along a breakwater and exclaiming "Look at me! Look at me!"

V

Having opened the envelopes and slit the circulars which Amaryllis had brought me, I saw that the letters were not urgent, and that the circulars came from persons who imagined that I would join "The Peace-at-Any-Price Union," "The Christian Communist Association," the "Be Fair to Germany Alliance," or "The Anti-British-Tyranny Group." Any man who had written a book or a play was assumed by our pithless intellectuals to be automatically in favour of all these half-witted, if well-intentioned, "movements."

When their manifestoes were safely in the waste-paper basket, I returned to a consideration of my own symptoms. Had I, or had I not, "Blackwood's"? Hearing that I had not even caught up with Manet or Bernard Shaw, most diagnosticians would have thrown up their hands, admitting that my case was hopeless. I took heart, nevertheless, from the fact that nobody now breathing could delight more than I do in the brilliant loveliness of Aubrey Beardsley's work. Remember, said I to my imagined opponent, Beardsley, though dead and gone, is not of earlier date than Shaw and is even later in time than those Impressionists who in my view sought to make pictures perform what pictures were never meant to do—very much like dogs playing football in a music-hall turn. Yes,

yes—Monet, Manet, Lautrec, and the rest of them—were they possibly no more than performing seals? Could it be that the true aim of painting had been achieved in the sixteenth century? And that subsequent painters (of any importance) were like fish in the grass, frantically proclaiming how vigorously their art still lived?

I did not wish that the arts might remain at a standstill: yet I felt that young men, desperately intent upon asserting themselves, did, generation after generation, delude their followers, like gaseous will-o'-the-wisps, into mere marshland. These poets and painters who were so strikingly at odds with the normal seemed to me like those persons who have not realised that charm is innate and unconscious. Again, I had known three or four middle-aged men and women who prided themselves upon having a peculiar gift for getting on well with the young. They invariably cut a somewhat ridiculous figure, not least in the eyes of the generation which they were so diligently flattering; and at once I perceived that timid and elderly reviewers who dare not say that some new movement is rootless and misleading are no better than sycophantic humbugs. A man is not a fool because he is fifty.

By this time I was feeling considerably reassured: and when I considered that no generation in any country to-day is likely to produce more than one writer, one painter, one composer —or just possibly two—of permanent interest, I became practically certain that, after all, far from contracting "Blackwood's" at the age of twenty, I might merely have kept my head. I looked at the vast growth of prose and poetry which had burgeoned in England during my lifetime, and although they had enjoyed their vogues I could not believe that Ezra Pound, D. H. Lawrence, Arnold Bennett, Aldous Huxley or even Bernard Shaw would stick in the memory of Englishmen if Wilfred Scawen Blunt and Meredith himself were already authors whom nobody perused. There was Yeats, of course —Yeats who might stay for good, as he adumbrated, "with Landor and with Donne," but in my day there had been, I surmised, only one Englishman whom we ought to call a "great" writer.

I rose and went to the shelf on which I kept my favourite and lifelong books. I came back to my chair with *The Dynasts* in my hand; and meaning only to re-read a scene or two, I continued reading until midnight and without troubling much about the sirens which warned all silent London that German bombers were approaching.

VIII
AN UNFORTUNATE ADVENTURESS

AN actor once told me that his life had gone agley because, though he looked like Hamlet, he had not Hamlet's intelligence. He had been driven, in short, to live up to his fine and melancholy face. In the same way, people have always assumed that I am a lover of first editions, an indigo-blue tory, and a formidable authority upon wines. The truth is that I care nothing for first editions, that I applaud the notion of aristocracy but detest the behaviour of most aristocrats, and that my long slavery to gout has prevented me from acquiring the most elementary knowledge of wine.

However, very soon after the death of Arnold Bennett, Susan Carwell—a wild, impulsive, half-Irish lady who had known him for years—rang me up and said, "I want you to dine here on Tuesday. Harry Jonas, the painter, is coming, and I know you like him, and so is another painter—Bruce Deverell. Oh, you know him too! All the better. And by the way, dear, now that Arnold is dead, I shall want you to see that I get the right wines for my little cellar." I protested that I did not know one château from another. "Nonsense," retorted Susan, "everybody knows that you have the finest palate in London." Twenty years earlier, in 1913, I had sipped my ultimate glass of port, and the memory of it was now a poetic emotion recollected in tranquillity.

Susan herself and Harry Jonas were guarantees of a happy and memorable evening, but every dinner-party was to me a romance and an adventure. I would go to it as the Third Son in a fairy-story set forth to find a fortune. Men and women whom I did not know would assemble in Susan's drawing-room, like queer persons in a tale by Somerset Maugham who convene in a Government guest-house away in the swampiest outpost of the Malay States. They would be my fellow-inhabitants of this glittering universe, co-dreamers with me in the dream-story which would be called the earlier twentieth-century, and each of them would be carrying about with him the experiences of thirty, forty, or fifty years. I had shared those years, and it seemed odd that I should not know my fellow-annalists.

Susan placed me at the far end of the table, opposite herself, a pretty compliment which I much appreciated. To balance the three men—Harry Jonas, Bruce Deverell, and myself—our hostess had invited two women. One, I report with shame, has left no mark on my memory. The other, an American blonde, a Mrs. Linnet Frain, had cause for remembering that dinner-party, and perhaps remembers it still.

I guessed that she was about thirty-six. She had April blue eyes, but there were lines underneath them. Her hair was the colour of dry sand, so pale an ochre as almost to be silver. Time had not spoiled her figure: and I noticed that her arms had the shapeliness which comes of use. She had been, in fact, an expert swimmer. I noticed also that her breasts, dimly apprehensible despite her satin dress, were tip-tilted and provocatively formed.

There was no need to "take care" of Linnet, if I may use that pretty American phrase. Bruce, having applied himself enthusiastically to Susan's Lafitte, hardly left Mrs. Frain for a minute, and yet I did just have time to learn that, like so many of her countrywomen, she dabbled in fortune-telling and astrology. For the rest, we pretended not to notice the idyll of the nymph and the shepherd which proceeded in a corner of Susan's drawing-room, and we went on to discuss the newest plays, the newest novels, and that queer, pale, morbid and parasitic poetry which had already come up like a growth of toadstools. Then, a little before midnight, Harry Jonas and I thanked Susan and proceeded to walk through the dry, cold night towards the West End. "And what do you make," said I to Harry, "of that Mrs. Frain?" He replied, in his brown-velvet voice, "I've met her before. She's an unsuccessful adventuress." "Isn't that," I asked him, "the woefullest of all careers?"

I heard no more of Mrs. Frain for the best part of a week. Then she rang up and, speaking with her pleasant Arkansas drawl, asked if she might come to see me at once. "You know Bruce Deverell," she drawled, "and so you can kind of direct me." When she arrived, at tea-time, I was greatly charmed by her New-World candour. "You see," she said, "I'm a very rare creature, by your English standards. . . . I'm a poor American, believe it or not. And I'm also entirely in love with your beautiful England, especially your London. I've been married," she went on, "only I didn't kind of care about Mr. Frain's approach to the sex-problem, so I guess I've not seen him for the last fifteen years. Maybe I'm not hard enough for life in the States. Maybe I'm too dreamy. Maybe. Sometimes I think I'll end up in a Tibetan nunnery, and other times I think I'd be wasting my looks. Oh, I realise I'm no front-row glory-girl, but seems I've still a twilight charm. Take your friend, Bruce Deverell. After that dinner he came up to me and he said 'Linnet, I don't have to use your surname. I've fallen in love with your jolly little pouting breasts, and you're going to be my love.'"

"And," I asked, "are you?" Her answer seemed to throw a beamlight upon her unsuccessful career. "I shall be—to-night," said Linnet, "and I'm praying so hard that he will really enjoy me." Then she added, "D'you think he'll go on caring —afterwards? That's what I really came to ask you about."

"Artists," I mumbled, "artists . . ."

"And they're the only men," said Linnet, sadly, "who are worth loving."

It must have been a fortnight later that I next heard of Mrs. Frain, and much may happen in a fortnight. Bruce Deverell walked into my Albany room, his eyes abnormally dilated. He

chucked his hat on to the green sofa, snatched a cigarette,
prowled up and down the big room, and began talking to me
as though I were another aspect of himself. "She's damned
pretty," he muttered, "—Linnet, I mean. You remember
Linnet. And in bed, as a lover, she's like a Scarlatti minuet,
a Herrick flower-poem. Fair daffodils, etc. Something of
Conder, too—a fanlike woman. And another thing . . . I've
always heard that rapture transforms a woman, makes her look
half her age. Well, I've never seen that, until now. My dear
chap, when I'm loving her, I can see what Linnet looked like
when she was twenty."

"It all sounds charming," I said, encouragingly.

"She's been running up bills," Bruce added, "twenty-eight
pounds with her wine merchant. Of course, I don't mind that.
All women imagine that money is like dew—something which
appears every morning. Anyway, we can't let an American
lady be dunned by a beastly London wine merchant. . . ."

"Then what," I said, "is the matter?"

"She's taking it too damned seriously," said Bruce. "I went
to her yesterday evening, and she told me that she had found
the ideal home for us—the very cutest little eighteenth-century
house, and the rent a mere five hundred guineas a year. . . ."
(Poor Linnet, I thought, why don't you hitch your wagon to
some steadfast adulterer from the world of big business?)
"I've just come from her flat," Bruce was saying. "She wasn't
angry—that's the devil of it—but she says that I don't care
enough for her, and so it had better end. A bit thick, you know.
I liked her. As an odalisk, she was just what I wanted."

"Bruce," I said, "she has definitely handed you your hat
and gloves?"

"Because I won't set up house with her—yes!" I told him
that I thought he would hear from her again.

He did—four days later. Ringing me up in a state of wild
agitation, he exclaimed, "I know all about the suicide-threat,
but this is a new one on me. I asked Linnet to dine with me in
Soho. She said 'Not dinner.' I asked 'Why not?' And she
answered 'I've not eaten anything, honey, since we said good-
bye, last Thursday, but don't you bother about that. It's a way

out, and I'm perfectly calm: only, of course, a little faint and weak! . . .' What do you think?" cried Bruce.

"The newest form of hunger-strike," I suggested, "'Love me or I'll starve.' . . . What would Lysistrata have said?"

"She won't see anybody but you," Bruce persisted. "Will you go and see her? I simply must know what's happening."

Of course I made an appointment, and duly called upon Mrs. Frain at her Mayfair flat a little before seven o'clock. It goes without saying that, at my age, I had known women who had threatened to drown or to shoot themselves in order to keep hold of their restless husbands but—and here was the point— I had known two women who had not been play-acting. And Linnet Frain—self-exiled, a little faded, and now at the end of her resources—might, I felt, actually starve to death in a sort of pseudo-mystical exaltation.

As I knocked on the door of her flat, I observed two bottles of milk, ominously full. She opened the door, and I perceived that she was wearing a dressing-gown. I could see also an uncanny brilliance in her blue eyes.

"Come right in," said Mrs. Frain, almost tenderly, "there's nothing to make a fuss about. Bruce doesn't kind of love me as I long to be loved, that's all. You can't blame him, now can you? And I've no prospects. I shan't grow younger and I shan't grow prettier; and, as you know, I'm not in the least afraid of the Next World. In fact, I look forward to a new start."

"You can hardly expect me," said I, "to go and have dinner at my club while I leave you to starve. . . ."

"Why not?" she drawled. "A day or two more, and I'll be in the vision-world of Santa Teresa, and this little body'll just gradually fade away."

"You're not strong enough," I suggested, "to come for a short walk?"

"My legs have gone all scrimbly," she answered, "like after 'flu."

"Very well, then," I rejoined. "I am going to take you out so that you can say farewell to this charming old London which you have loved so deeply. While you go and dress, I will wait here and read a book." She obeyed me so quietly, so automatically, that I was surprised; and during her absence I found myself wholly unable to decide whether she was shamming or in earnest, whether she had will enough to go through with her scheme to its terrifying end or whether she would be thankful if somebody were to throw her a lifebelt. No, not for the life of me could I be certain, and on the whole I believed that this once-fair woman was perfectly sincere. She did mean to starve but, I reflected, if she is, all the same, as Jonas pronounced, "an unsuccessful adventuress," may it not be that she has lacked the fierce will-power which makes for success? And if that were true, it ought to be possible to break down her will-towards-death.

"Thank you," I said when she returned; and very pretty she looked in her old-fashioned furs. "The taxi is waiting. I thought that you could not walk very far."

We got into our taxi, and Linnet looked wistfully, I thought, at the neat bricks of the Queen Anne houses which we passed; and when we had caught a glimpse of St. James's Square, she sighed, "How I loved that patch when I first came to London . . ." At length we arrived at the Automobile Club where, after we had severally discarded our outermost envelopes, I steered her, half-dreaming as she was, into the great dining-room, brilliant with lights and noisy with a babble which obliterated the music of the string quartet.

My strategy would have done credit to Caesar Borgia. It was entirely successful. "Linnet," I said, "it is now eight-forty-three, and I am more than a little hungry. And do you not observe how the waiters are beginning to glance at our empty plates? I hate to look absurd, but I shall do so unless you will come to my aid. In a word, my dear, I am not going to eat anything at all unless you will eat the same quantity of the same dish. Do we start with hors d'oeuvres or with *sole à la bonne femme*?"

"I can't eat, Clifford," she said, almost piteously, like a General who cannot bear to give up his sword.

"Here's the waiter," I muttered testily. "He must guess nothing. I can't possibly tell him that we're sitting here for the fun of the thing. Linnet, my good name, my dignity, my reputation as a sane man, are in your hands." Then, turning to the waiter, the small dark one who loves music, I said "Sole for two, and a bottle of a hundred-and-eighty-five."

Such, then, was Linnet Frain's evening breakfast, nor did I see her again for perhaps three weeks. She invited me, I remember, to "take a cup of your English tea," and of course I accepted in order to see if my cure was progressing. She floated towards me, cooing, "I want you to know Mr. Florian Choose, the great occultist. He's from Canada. Meet Mr. Florian Choose. . . ." I learned soon, from his own confession, that Mr. Choose was "the only man in the Western Hemisphere who completely understands the yoga-systems of the East, and," he added, "Mrs. Frain was predestined to be my assistant." She ought, I judged, to be able to underprop her bank balance for several months to come.

Do I seem to have treated her anguish too lightly? If so, it is only because all's well if it ends well. And yet, even older now than I was in those days, I still believe that Linnet Frain was capable, if she had not been deflected, of starving to death in the West End of London. Born as an American citizen, she had not the harsh egoism which American life demands. Too fastidious for her slap-dash husband, she was also too gentle, too loving, for success in the world of free-love. She misfired on all cylinders, and I could not help thinking that she ought, by rights, to have been an odalisk in the hareem of some poetry-loving Turk or Egyptian.

Six years later, Mrs. Frain was still alive. She sent me a Christmas card. It portrayed the warm windows of an English inn, with deep snow outside.

IX

SHAKESPEARE AND SMITH

I HAVE heard two old cricketers in the pavilion at Lansdown begin a discussion about port as I led my team at half-past eleven on to the field, and have heard them still discussing port when we trooped back, two hours later, to enjoy the luncheon interval. It is in much the same spirit, I fancy, that Leon M. Lion and I, two lifelong lovers of poetry, seldom spend an evening together without comparing impressions of England's vintage verse: only, we have this advantage over those who recollect the flavour of bygone ports, that our nectar is imperishable and we are able, in consequence, at any moment to go down into the cellar and to come back fondly nursing a bottle of sparkling Swinburne or nicely matured Keats or rich old crusted Spenser.

And on the evening which I now have in mind I knew that Leon was in for a treat. We had agreed to have an early supper at Scott's and then to see a performance of *A Midsummer Night's Dream* in the open-air theatre at Regent's Park; and I remember that particular performance with special clearness because it gave me the second of two ideas concerning literature which, though perhaps obvious to other men, came to me as happy surprises. The fact is, then, that a good many years earlier I had picked up a faded copy of a certain book of poems, and that this book, which was a second edition, contained press-notices of the poet's work when it had first appeared. He received such an astonishing ovation that I wonder at myself for having delayed so long before really examining his verse.

"Well, Leon," I said, as he came into the room, holding out both hands in his warm-hearted way, "we needn't go out for another five minutes, and I've a magnificent *apéritif* to offer you. . . ."

"What, my dear fellow," he replied, "could be nobler than your sherry?"

"It goes with the sherry," I assured him. "Here is the sherry—good luck to you! And here is a batch of press-notices that might turn any man's head."

"Wait, wait! Who is it? A new poet?"

"No. He died in 1867 . . ."

"Tell me his name."

"Smith."

"Smith, Smith. . . . I must try to remember that name."

"I have always been interested," I went on, "in Alexander Smith because Tennyson wrote him an encouraging letter, and Smith, in order to impress a group of friends, used the letter as a spill for his pipe."

"Good heavens! . . . But 1867, you say?"

"Yes, that's when he died. His first book of poems appeared, I think, in 1853; that is to say, three years after Wordsworth's death. Tennyson had become poet laureate. Rossetti, who was then twenty-five, must have noticed this literary meteor, and even Swinburne, although he was only sixteen, probably read the book with juvenile excitement. As for the world of action and affairs, our bewhiskered ancestors were still unaware that there would soon be a war in the Crimea and a Mutiny in India."

"You have set the stage very nicely, my dear boy. Now, for the poetry."

"No," I responded, "we'll keep that until after 'the Dream' is over."

"Just for a few minutes—then we must go—I want to whet your appetite by asking you to go back eighty-five years and to stroll into your club and to glance through half a dozen of the most influential journals."

"I am in my favourite club-chair," said Leon. "I am stroking my long Crimean beard, and I am wondering what the deuce these demnition reviewin' fellers have to say about young Smith."

Picking up the faded green volume, I began to read from the front pages. "There was," I explained, "a paper called *The Nonconformist*. It said, 'Let the praise sound extravagant as it may, Alexander Smith is a finer poet than Keats, in the very qualities in which Keats was finest.' The *Weekly News and*

6

Chronicle referred to 'a diction which, in its mingled force and flexibility, is fully equal to the most varied purposes of the most world-wide poetry."

My friend's monocle dropped. I could see that he was impressed. "*The Manchester Examiner*," I continued, "described Smith as 'a man who has won for himself'—at twenty-three, mind you!—'a place in the rank of living poets: confined, we are afraid, at this moment almost to Tennyson, the Brownings, and himself.' . . . That seems a little unkind to Matthew Arnold."

"Go on, go on!" urged Leon, enthusiastically lighting a second cigar.

"The *Liverpool Standard* records that 'already paeans of praise are ringing through the length and breadth of the land, at the advent of one whom we certainly believe to be the greatest poet Scotland has ever produced.'"

Leon got up. He began to prowl up and down, and to pull faster at his cigar than it deserved.

"The *Glasgow Citizen* said that this book 'contains passages of almost unsurpassed beauty and power.' The *Leader* states that 'Alexander Smith is a poet and a man of unmistakable genius'; the *Daily News* also speaks of 'indisputable marks of genius'; the *Westminster Review* cried out that there is 'not a page of this volume on which we cannot find some novel image, some Shakespearian felicity of expression, or some striking simile'; the *Literary Gazette* opened, almost timidly, that 'since Tennyson, no poet has come before the public with the same promise,' but the *Spectator* makes handsome amends by saying, 'It is to the earlier work of Keats and Shelley alone that we can look for a counterpart in richness of fancy and force of expression to the *Life Drama*.' The *Nation* sets a crown upon this extraordinary chorus of praise by declaring quite simply that 'a new poet takes his place in the literature of England.'"

"Well!" exclaimed Leon. "After all that, let's have a poem or two." But I denied him. It was time to get our snack—if snack it could be called—but I begged him to come back after the play and to savour this belauded verse for himself."

II

Thanks to Mr. Willett, the sun was only westering and had not gone down, like "the good ship *Immortality*," when we made our way to "the Park," and fortunately the day had been melting-hot and the early night promised a comfortable temperature for the assembled audience. How many times, during the years when Sydney Carroll was presenting plays of everlasting beauty in the romantic setting provided by the lawns and the flower-beds and the tall, graceful trees of Queen Mary's Garden—how many times did I make one in that audience, happy in a degree which I have not often attained—happy because I was hearing English wielded with the utmost ease and with the unconscious "force and flexibility" that comes natural to genius; happy because for two hours or so I could sink back into the latter half of Queen Elizabeth's long reign, and watch plays which have never been surpassed unfold before me in all their mingled stateliness and mirth; and happy, too—on this occasion—to hear the master-music of young Mendelssohn float out into the twilight and weave a second loveliness into the matchless texture of those ancient lines which the players were speaking. For that little stretch of time I was free to forget an age that I never relished, and to live again in a time when Englishmen expressed their minds in vigorous and inventive speech, were not ashamed to be patriots, dared to weep if the cause were strong enough and yet could put to shame our thin-lipped phantom of their Elizabethan laughter. And sometimes, too, if Mendelssohn vanished away among the darkening shrubbery and Leslie French were to sing a Shakespeare lyric to music which also came from that gallant epoch, then my delight made up to me for innumerable sorrows of the heart and disappointments of ambition. The only tears which have come into my eyes since I was a frantic child are the tears which too much beauty must evoke if beauty is to be recognised at all.

A theatre manager is either a bit of a buccaneer or else he ought never to have ventured upon the high seas of drama. Leon and Carroll were experienced buccaneers of the theatre, and it was merely natural that after the first act Sir Walter

Raleigh (as it were) should pay a visit to Sir Francis Drake. They stayed a long time in the cabin; and I was alone, or so I thought, when the play continued. The summer light was now gone, and as the stars reappeared—almost hesitantly—in the great depths above us, cunning electricians made the scene in front of us look as if it were indeed an enchanted garden where any strange adventure was not only possible, but to be expected. And never did it seem more obvious that Titania would throw her exquisite beauty at an ass-headed weaver, and even the little whispering sigh of a breeze among the surrounding bushes seemed only to be saying, "What a strange fantasy to have entered the imagination of a charming, companionable Elizabethan from Warwickshire. . . . Do you think it might have a secret meaning? Do you, do you?"

But I was already preoccupied with a queer sensation. As I watched the unfolding of that play, so ingenious in its devices for sustaining interest and pleasure, I suddenly realised that in a certain sense I was writing it as I listened: and I thought, "Why, the whole joy of seeing a lovely play or of reading a fine novel comes precisely from the fact that we recreate it as we go! We have none of the anguish that most authors know while they work: we have only their residuum of delight when they see the work leap into life. Everybody who watches a Shakespeare play with appreciation is looking over his shoulder as he builds that play—is, in a sense and just for the time being, Shakespeare himself! We should not enjoy books and plays if we did not become their authors as we read them."

This notion excited me as if it were bound to prove equally exciting to other people. Moreover, it brought back to my mind another simple-startling notion which had quickened me many years earlier. I had been wondering what could possibly have been the emotion or thought or desire which had caused the world's greatest authors to pre-imagine their greatest works. "Alfred," wrote Lady Tennyson, "is looking for a new subject." We know that Sir Philip Sidney had also hunted for a subject, and that his Muse had told him to look in his heart, and write. Suddenly, however, I thought I had discerned a more definite source of inspiration for at least half the books which a staggering world still continues to shoulder. "Write what you wish you could read," would make, I fancied, no poor prescription. "Give yourself what you want," I continued, "and if the world does not want it also, you must put up with that. In any case, you may try your hardest to write the book which you would most like to read, but of course it will come out as a poor, pallid simulacrum of that first radiant idea. But still—it's a sound prescription, and I shall say to any young man who asks for advice, 'Write the book which you'd like to read.' That is certainly what William Morris did when he composed his long, dreamy prose-romances."

An aged gentleman, silver-haired and silver-bearded, had unobtrusively taken the deck-chair to the right of my own: and now Leon came back and, smoking another cigar, reclined into the deck-chair to my left. We were waiting to be re-enchanted by the play as presented, with no silly effort to give it an up-to-date interest, by that reborn frequenter of the Bank-side, Robert Atkins, a very obvious Elizabethan. And I suggested to Leon that the quickest way to appreciate the unique wonder of a great work of art is to say to ourselves, "That canvas was once a blank: there was a time when not a word of 'the Dream' had been put on to paper. All this glory—of paint or of words and character-portrayal—came out of nothing. . . ."

At this moment the silvery gentleman on my right interposed. "Excuse me," he said, "I recognise Mr. Lion, and I cannot help overhearing some of your conversation. Has it ever occurred to you, gentlemen, that Shakespeare must have returned to his writing-table, day after day, for at least several weeks? People take him for granted. They take the plays for granted. They don't stop to think that these plays had to be laboriously written out with a squeaky quill and in that cumbersome Elizabethan script. Now, Shakespeare must sometimes have started cold, and I wish my old friend Frank Harris had applied his bull's-eye lantern intelligence to that interesting theme. For instance, can we not divine how Shakespeare must have lost touch with the story of *Romeo and Juliet* when, coming back (as I guess) from a spree of three or four days with some of his boon-companions, he had to sit down to that table, pick up his quill and, suffering slightly from a hang-over, set the play moving once more with the ground-out couplets of poor old Friar Laurence—you know—

> The grey-eyed morn smiles on the frowning night,
> Chequering the eastern clouds with streaks of light.

and the rest of it. "Oh," said the old gentleman, "I fully realise that these lines have been much admired: but they are the work of a writer who is getting up steam . . . and I could cite several more passages of the same slack quality. The wonder is that so often he seems to have started straight off with something ever-memorable—as if he took up his quill and dipped it into immortal poetry, not into mere ink. For instance, the opening speech of *Twelfth Night*! Is it conceivable that any man could come in from lunch and immediately write those lines? No, gentlemen, no! Believe me, Shakespeare had written them several months earlier, while listening to music, and there they were—to his hand. . . ."

"This is all very interesting," said Leon.

"And do you suppose," continued our mysterious enthusiast, "that the poet when he was writing *Hamlet* stopped when he came to page 23 or page 48, and, putting the play out of his mind, there and then composed the famous soliloquies? That is not how authors work. Gentlemen, those soliloquies were written separately and were afterwards incorporated in the play. They may possibly be the contribution of the Earl of Oxford, for I think it possible that Oxford, well known as a patron of the drama, may have asked Shakespeare to use certain set-speeches, just as Hamlet provides the Players with some lines which he wants them to adopt. Shakespeare of Stratford was the skilled professional playwright and the unparalleled poet, but Oxford may well have had his moments of amateurish and intermittent authorship. "Or"—the old gentleman was quite irrespressible—"take Mercutio's speech about Queen Mab. It's absurdly out of character. It does not fit in with the flippant, sword-swinging personality of Mercutio. It is, gentlemen, a piece of intaglio. Shakespeare had to use it, and I think—once again—that perhaps it was presented to him by Oxford. But——"

Trumpeters came on to the greensward, and they trumpeted, and, in the light of the rising moon and of the stars, that old wild fantasy, first born in an Elizabethan brain, proceeded once more, after three hundred years of change, to charm its latest audience: nor could I help marvelling that a play of this type, and poetry of this sustained loveliness, must have been acceptable in the London theatres of 1600. What manager, I wondered, would accept the manuscript now?

As the night deepened I became more confident that our joy in a work of art comes from a process of re-creating it. When we hear a sonata by Brahms, we become Brahms, and when we look at Rembrandt's portrait of the "Old Woman," whose fragile body can hardly cohere for another six months, we ourselves are manipulating the dear old master's brushes.

III

The performance was over, and doing my best to offer a stiff upper-lip to the world, I also did my best to conceal the beauty tears which, I must admit, were brimming my eyes. That miracle of poetry and effective "theatre" still challenged a twentieth-century which had already disgraced itself a dozen times over.

We got up. I said to our anonymous enthusiast, "Having told you our own names, may we ask for yours?"

He answered, "Think of me as Mr. W. H. . . . You will not be far wrong. Now, your friend," he continued, indicating Leon, "has not your intuitions. He still believes in science as an alternative to religion. . . ."

"I cannot quite descend to a science," interjected Leon, "but I can rise to a superstition!"

"Gentlemen," said Mr. W. H., who was obviously a well-preserved octogenarian, "we shall not meet again. I shall see my last of this painful, though fascinating, world in the small hours of October the 22nd. How do I know? By dint of having studied astrology for the last fifty-nine years. . . . And I say to you," he said, fixing me with an Ancient Mariner's eye, "that I want you to carry away this evening one idea, if only one. It is a tremendously deep-plunging idea, and people will not pay any attention to it until two or three centuries have passed by: but somehow I want—as it were—to bequeath it to a man who is likely to outlive me by twenty or thirty years. . . ."

"What is it?" I asked. The auditorium was practically empty. The catering staff, and Mr. Landstone, and even the actors and actresses were beginning to pack up. "The soul and life," said Mr. W. H., "are not one and the same. It was natural for primitive man to suppose that they were. That is why the Greek word for 'soul' is also the Greek word for 'breath.' The truth is just the very opposite. Life is a fierce, passionate, selfish, unscrupulous energy. You can see it at work all through historians' history. Life, believe me, is a horrible, pitiless, and abominable force. It is another name for what our forefathers termed the Devil. But the soul is a little weak, tender, faintly sprouting entity. It's very hall-mark is that it denies the violent claims of the life-force. The soul, my dear sir, is having a damned hard time in getting through at all; but sometimes it does, and that is when we see a man upsetting the instinct of mere life, and 'laying down his life for his friend.' Good-bye —God bless you!" said the octogenarian, and walked out of our lives.

IV

So we two went back to Albany, my friend being curious to learn more about Alexander Smith and I just as eager to share my discovery. "One of those press-notices," remarked Leon, "gave high praise to a piece called 'A Life Drama.' Have you got it?"

"Yes—in this book," I assured him.

"And is it any good at all?" asked Leon, accepting a cigar. "I can't believe somehow that such a crowd of reviewers could be wrong."

"You shall judge for yourself."

We settled down to a quick study of the book. "Scene One," I said, "shows Walter at 'Midnight' in 'an Antique Room,' and he is reading a poem which he has just written.

After this, jumping up, he expresses a wish to give himself to 'Poesy':

> As Hero gave her trembling sighs to find
> Delicious death on wet Leander's lip. . . .

"Did you say 'wet'?" Leon asked.

"Now, Scene Two shows Walter asleep under a tree. A Lady enters 'with a fawn'—yes, a fawn—whose name, rather surprisingly, is Flora. 'Halt, Flora, halt!' the Lady commands, and then, seeing Walter, exclaims, a little crudely, perhaps:

> Ha! what is this? A bright and wandered youth,
> Thick in the light of his own beauty, sleeps
> Like young Apollo, in his golden curls. . . .
>
> A lovely youth,
> With dainty cheeks and ringlets like a girl,
> And slumber-parted lips 'twere sweet to kiss!

Indeed, she is so much impressed by our pink and golden poet that we hear no more of Flora. Walter wakes up and, not in the least surprised, indulges at once in a spate of self-pity, his besetting weakness. 'Fair lady,' he almost sobs, 'in my dream

> Methought I was a weak and lonely bird,
> In search of summer, wandered on the sea,
> Toiling through mists, drenched by the arrowy rain,
> Struck by the heartless winds. . . .

and so on. The Lady urges Walter to recite one of his poems, and he literally sings a highly unsingable poem. The Lady was impressed. 'You should give the world,' she murmured, 'such delicious thoughts as these,' and Walter, thus encouraged, confesses his poetic ambitions. I am surprised, since we are in the midst of the crinoline-and-croquet period, that the Lady should ask, provocatively:

> Wilt write of some young wanton of an isle
> Whose beauty so enamoured hath the sea,
> It clasps it ever in its summer arms
> And wastes itself away on it in kisses?

Walter, you will be glad to hear, has nobler projects."

"And Scene Three?" said Leon, not quite sure of his verdict.

"Unimportant. Walter is back in his Antique Room. It is enough to tell you that Walter would now prefer to win the Lady by his verses

> Than immortality in twenty worlds . . .

"Scene Four shows Walter and the Lady on the bank of a river, and Walter, still reciting, says of his hero that

> He gave her lands; she paid him with herself,

and what do you suppose the Lady comments upon so bald a statement? She says:

> Most fit reward!
> A poet's love should ever thus be paid . . .

and, really, one feels a little impatient with Walter for not taking so broad a hint, but even now he is not sure that he has been a success, and so he goes to the labour of writing a long allegorical poem about a haughty Princess and her Indian slave-lad. She calls him 'Leopard,' and at one moment she refers to

> The blood that purples in these azure veins,
> Rich'd with its long course through a hundred earls,

which, if my computation is right, carries her ancestry back to the age of Homer. . . ."

"But what of the story?" said Leon, impatiently, "don't keep interrupting it."

I gave him another whisky-and-soda. Then I reported that the Lady was unable to marry Walter because 'within a month my bridal bells will make a village glad': and, prophesying a sad future for the poet and an early death for herself, she wanders away. . . ."

"Feeling a little sore, perhaps?" interrupted Leon.

"She had every right to be cross with him," I admitted, "for no man can expect a Lady to offer herself more frankly. However, crushed by this failure, Walter now rambles down a 'Rural Lane' until he encounters, as he puts it, 'one of my peasants': a curiously late use of that word in English. . . ."

"Keep to the story, please", said Leon.

"The peasant likes being alive and proudly displays one of

his children to the moody master: nor is it strange that 'the Child looks fearfully up at him,' for Walter, playing Hamlet or Werther or Byron, somewhat crudely says to the Peasant:

> O die, man, die!
> Get underneath the earth for very shame.

V

I put the book down and fetched myself a drink. "It seems really almost impossible," murmured Leon, "that all those critics could have announced that here was one of our great poets. . . . And yet I dare say their grandchildren are doing just the same thing about some of our own young fashionable poets. Surely, though," he continued, "it isn't all quite so bad as the bits that you've exposed?"

"No," I confessed, "but even at twenty-two, and with the late lamented Wordsworth in his mind, no poet should have been able to write

> My heart is in the grave with her;
> The family went abroad . . ."

"But what happened to Walter?" persisted Leon, looking about for more matches.

"He proceeds to indulge his vein of wild melancholy when suddenly 'Enter Edward, unobserved' . . ."

"Who is he?" said Leon, sharply, as though I were adding another salary to the cast.

"Up till now," I replied, "he has not been mentioned, but I can tell you that he is a man of law, that Walter regards him as a soulless clod and that, nevertheless, he listens to the poet's ravings far into the night. He is a modern; he admires the new railways

> That bring the country butter up to town,

but, clod that he is, Edward can do little except listen cynically to his voluble and humourless friend. After that, Walter, so far as I can make out, goes to the dogs, but not too reprehensibly. We meet him at midnight on a bridge where he encounters a belated prostitute; and after some gloomy comparisons of her life and his, Walter, possibly remembering a line in 'The White Devil,' exclaims:

> My heart's on fire by hell, and on I drive
> To outer blackness, like a blazing ship,

and then further astounds the poor girl by abruptly 'rushing away.' He returns to his garden. A little later, Edward is sitting with a new character named Charles, kindly inquiring for news of the poet: and Charles reports that

> when the moon
> Was waning dim upon the edge of morn,
> Still sat he writing, thoughtful-eyed and pale . . .

I don't know what Charles was doing at that time of night. He goes on to say:

> And, as of yore, round his white temples reeled
> His golden hair, in ringlets beautiful.

"This Charles," commented Leon, "appreciated him much more than the loutish Edward. I can see that."

"Anyway, they all meet at the country-house of a 'Mr. Wilmot,' who owns a large amount of land and a pretty daughter whose name is Violet. Walter is sadly unsociable and sits glooming by himself while Edward and Charles, at Mr. Wilmot's bidding, try to ease the situation by trolling out fairly jovial songs. And Violet, sensitive to the gloom in one corner of the parlour, sings in a more sentimental vein. Walter, having no heart for song, disappoints Charles by telling a long lugubrious tale. However, though the house-party must have been trying for Mr. Wilmot, it achieved its purpose. Walter and Violet 'got together'; and although the poet has now realised that

> Never henceforward can I hope to drain
> The rapture of a lifetime at a gulp

every subsequent poet will appreciate the significance of this dialogue:

WALTER: Have you read my book?
VIOLET: I have.
WALTER: It is enough. . . .

but I do admit, Leon, that the idealistic love-talk which closes the wobbly and bloated poem is not without beauty."

VI

It was close upon two in the morning when Leon and I, having finished our morning-caps, went down the Rope Walk, intent upon finding for him a taxi. The lesson of Alexander Smith was not lost upon either of us; and half-way along the Walk, Leon stopped, recited a few lines from Shakespeare, and said, "So Smith and his friends were named the Spasmodic School. How, my dear boy, would you name our latest batch of quite unsingable 'singers'?"

At fifteen I had resented being called a "child"; at fifty I was always charmed if somebody addressed me as "my dear boy": and thus inspired, I answered, "Finding most of them shapeless and unintelligible, I should call our fashionable poets from Eliot onwards the Ectoplasmic School. For instance, there is that poem called 'The Flight of the Margarine . . .'"

"Ha!" cried Leon, resuming his walk toward a taxi, "could there possibly be a better description of ectoplasm, m-m-m? . . . But as for Smith the rocket, and Smith the stick, how do you explain them?"

"To-day's paper," I replied, sententiously, "calls to us more urgently than the works of Montaigne or Plato. Yesterday's paper is spurned by everybody. In my time there was journalism, which dealt with current matters, and literature, which kept an eye on eternity: but Shaw, Wells, and Bennett have been such adroit journalists that people now value a book in terms of newspaper-interest."

"Well," he answered, with his Chinese smile, "you must, like Wells and Auden, enjoy your pet intolerances. . . . Good night!"

X

THE IMPORTANCE OF BEING VULGAR

MOST of us can remember certain mornings of boyhood, or even of early manhood, when the coming day promised so full a happiness that we could hardly endure the tedium of getting into our clothes—all the intricate fingerwork which braces and a necktie impose upon us, all that doing up of buttons and that subjugation of a refractory collar-stud. When these times of over-brimming happiness came to us we wanted to have done as quickly as possible with the mere ritual and routine of living. We were greedy, and feared to spill even a moment of such a day.

Some will associate this exuberance with the beginning of the holidays, and some, I expect, with the heady mead of a youthful honeymoon. For me that mood is most often connected with a lifelong enthusiasm for cricket. If my preparatory school—a loathsome compost of bullying and obscenity—was to play a match at two-thirty on a Saturday afternoon, I, a first-change bowler, could scarce believe the tardiness of that Saturday morning.

In later life we cannot expect to feast upon such perilous joy more than once or twice in a blue moon; and I call it perilous because of a mystical intuition that the woe and the joy in the world lie always at perfect balance—like the centrifugal and centripetal impulses which keep the earth spinning because they remain for ever equipollent. However, I had arrived (with incredulity) at my later forties when the gods presented to me another such day of nectar. Waking up at six-thirty and hearing the comfortable rumble of early morning London, I realised instantly that for once in a way I was not due to make war upon those infernal sibilants which riot like weeds all over the English language, but, on the contrary, was about to squander all the gold of a fine June day in watching a Test Match at Lord's; nor, I reflected, should I need to start early, or to shoulder my way through a throng of fellow-enthusiasts, or to queue up, like a tiny Bateman figure, at the dim end of St. John's Wood Road, or to be on tenterhooks for fear lest all the seats might be sold before I came at long last to the turnstile. I had, in a drawer and lying next to my very cheque-book, a plum-coloured ticket of admission and this would open for me those iron gates which commemorate the Happiest of All Men. And once inside, I had only to find my way to Charles Fry's all-welcoming grand-stand box.

I remembered, too, that in the evenings John Boynton Priestley was to dine with me in Albany, and that was another pleasure which I had in hand. Sometimes, it is true, we may see in *Country Life* a photograph of a Blue Persian snuggling up against a Yorkshire Terrier, but such harmony is unusual. I did not suppose that my visitor and I were destined to establish a myriad-faceted friendship, but Priestley had already earned three enviable reputations—as a stylish essayist who owed something to Hazlitt, as a best-selling novelist and, latterly, as a skilled and versatile playwright—so that I had plenty of cause for admiring him and for wishing to know him better. What's more, only a few weeks earlier I had seen with profound delight his bold and unique play, *Johnson Over Jordan*. This had been one of my major experiences in the theatre, and I wanted to offer the author my praise. Most of its professional critics missed the meaning of the play entirely, and babbled petulantly about its method as if it were merely a piece of entertainment; but perhaps we ought to have expected that they would prefer their customary diet of acorns. *Johnson* is much more than a mere play. It turned a West End theatre into a temple: it brought drama back to the origin of drama; it offered to all and sundry a breath-taking opportunity of passing unscathed through those bewildering experiences which (if we may trust the mysterious Thomas Taylor) will befall the soul in its earlier stages after the death of the body. Anyone who went to that theatre could learn something which a neophyte in the Eleusinian Mysteries could only have learned under guidance from an initiate and after drastic self-purification. Many who witnessed the play were probably unaware that they were rehearsing their own future—as they will act it after the major operation of death.

II

When I arrived at Lord's and had found Fry's enclosure, the game had yet to begin; and I saw in the corner of the box John Drinkwater, gazing dreamily at the green-golden sward. For some years I had felt that Drinkwater went about the world consciously impersonating English Literature, but of late he had seemed less Olympian in manner, though not less conventional in his literary judgments. On this day, he gave me two surprises. He murmured, for example, in his Warwickshire brogue and his attractive baritone, "Looking on at a game between England and Australia, in fine weather and among friends, is, I believe, my conception of the heavenly state." At this moment thirteen white-flannelled gladiators came forth from the bowels of the huge and hideous pavilion, and our host immediately directed his batman (or should I say his visir?) to distribute glasses of champagne and pyramids of exotic sandwiches. Perhaps it was the champagne which caused Drinkwater to give me a second surprise.

"You remember," he said, "that I adapted Mussolini's play about Napoleon . . .?"

"I remember it, yes. I saw it."

"Why," said the poet, "must he threaten to conquer Abyssinia? . . . It may not do any good, but yesterday I sent a long telegram, advising him to abandon the whole project." I remembered Dicky Bridport and those Indian agitators.

III

The Second European War was still some time ahead of us, and when Priestley arrived at my flat I could not know that its advent would bring him a fourth reputation—that of broadcasting more acceptably than anybody else to his war-worried countrymen. This man of protean talent became at a critical time the voice of a robust and unconquerable people.

We had not advanced beyond the lobster-mayonnaise when Priestley became, I thought, more than a little restless, and presently he remarked, while scooping out the contents of a claw, "The best writers are always a bit vulgar. They must have a streak of vulgarity. We ought not to be afraid of it. I've always felt," he continued, "that you'd be a better man and a better writer if only you were more vulgar."

"Vulgarity," I answered, sadly, "is like an earldom. You may be born to it and yet not deserve your luck. I will go further. I will say that, alas, unlike an earldom, it can never be achieved."

So long as Priestley and my other guests were with me, I accepted, with secret resignation, that all good men or writers are also good mixers, and share the tastes of the majority.

It was not until they were scattering homeward through the primrose lights of a London at peace that I began uneasily to wonder if, after all, most of our enduring writers had, in fact, been sufficiently vulgar. Late though it was, I could not tamely turn in; and, anxiously reviewing the hundreds of authors who stood on parade in my old bookcases, I was considerably abashed. I could remember no *bonhomie*, no jolly-good-fellowship, in Homer, Virgil, Dante, Calderon, Sir Thomas Browne ("God forbid!" I murmured, in passing), or in Dryden, Pope, Addison, Steele, Miss Austen, Baudelaire, Leopardi, Carducci. . . . And other names flocked to my fancy like clamouring gulls to a cliff, for it was not easy, somehow, to think of Plato, Landor, Henry James, and Yeats giving us a really thumping version of "A Jolly Good Fellow." On the other hand, there was a sound plebeian streak in Chaucer, Keats, and Dickens. Had not somebody gone so far as to say that Dickens could not present a gentleman or Cruickshank delineate one?

Still, there was truth in Priestley's tart criticism; and I fell into a reverie over my boyhood. I wondered how far, if at all, we choose our careers? At thirteen I looked like developing into a man of action. Certainly I prided my small self upon being practical and efficient, and it now seems to me that if, a few months later, I had admired a Navy man instead of a lady with a love of poetry, the whole of my life might have been different. Indeed, I still recognise that other potential self

7

who now lies buried under forty years of effort to write well. I suppose he twinkled a last finger-sign, like Till Eulenspiegel in Strauss's tone-poem, when, as a cricketer I figured as a hitter of sixes. . . . Yes, he died hard, that alternative me who might have lived if I had not become a writer of plays and books; and it may be that, listening over-acutely to every sound of every sentence, I have lost touch with the pulse of average humanity. The point remains, however, that not all of us can be writers who have a large public appeal, and that there may yet be some place for—shall we say?—an aristocratic writer.

No specialist is a well-informed man, and we ought always to keep all-roundness as our ideal. That characteristic is, let us reflect, precisely why Ancient Athens and Renaissance Italy remain with us as two of Europe's most splendid eras. For myself, I have found doctors to be perhaps the best of all companions. Their range is exceptionally broad, and since they need to be psychologists in at least a moderate degree, they are not like actors and actresses who cannot believe that anybody else is actually alive. Diplomatists hit my taste very happily, but this may be due to the pre-eminent diplomatist whom, of all those in his world, I have known best. I never left his house without giving thanks that in the midst of a raucous, roaring world there was a still centre of fine manners and rich culture. And I can listen delightedly to sailors, though they seldom grow up, and to farmers: but I never listen to farmers without recognising my extreme inferiority, for I have always known that all society is founded upon a triangle of farming, clothing, and building, and that the base of that triangle is farming. Lawyers, unfortunately, are disappointing. They ought to be as many-minded as doctors, but they very soon lose touch with erring humanity and become so circumspect that it is difficult to believe that they ever propagate their species.

If I were asked, then, what section of society I would choose were I in search of illuminating conversation, I would say "musicians, doctors, writers, and—when you can put salt upon their tailcoats—professional diplomatists." Priestley might have thought of me more highly if I had graduated upwards in the Foreign Office. It was too late. For better, for worse, in sickness or in health, I had chosen in boyhood to follow after the almost endless procession of English writers. An innate liking for subtlety and even for a high measure of court-liness, had, no doubt, exiled me as an inhabitant of a democratic age. Like all other out-of-fashion authors, I envy those authors who know that they are writing, not for ten readers, but for ten or a hundred thousand. It is fine to sail when the wind is favourable.

XI

EQUILATERAL

IN my time I have written and destroyed a good many diaries, ranging from an account of my turbid state of mind at the age of twenty-one to a quite recent record of wanderings in the United States and Scandinavia; but I am not nearly so resolute in respect of old engagement-books. Admittedly they have little or no use unless in a Court of Law eminent Counsel expects you to know what you were doing two years ago on the 18th November; and it must be a recognition of my weak-ness which causes me to hide these little pocket-books at the back of some drawer, under a heap of papers, and so to pretend that I have forgotten them. All the same, when I re-discovered an engagement-book for 1933, and observed that "Beryl" came to see me on April the 16th of that distant year, the whole uncommon story reformed itself in my imagination, and I was glad that I had reprieved that little book.

By 1933 Beryl had been married for eight years to Bob Philipsway—one of my earliest friends. He had been out in the Malay States, rubber-planting, for at least twelve years, and had met Beryl during a six months' holiday in England. They had gone out together and, judging from her letters, they spent four happy and remarkably prosperous years before coming home for good. I had always admired Bob Philipsway because he was enviably all-round, as a man should be. As a planter he had been astonishingly successful; he was now recognised as a shrewd fellow in the world of business; he excelled at half a dozen games; and he knew as much about the mysteries of music, literature, and painting as any layman has the right to know. He had, in fact, hardly been home for a few months before he became a Director in, I think, three large companies, including European Iron Supplies, Limited—vulgarly known as "Icicles."

II

Although her father was a Yorkshireman, I always thought of Beryl as being quite eighty per cent American. She had the epicene soul, the sexual coolness, which characterises so many young North American women and which, if accompanied by outstanding beauty, so often misleads the more passionate souls who incarnate in European bodies. She cannot have been entirely devoid of sexuality, but she had become so fastidious that she was almost out of touch with primitive instinct. She was obviously devoted to Bob, but rather as a moral life-partner, if I may so phrase my impression, than as an intellectual companion or an enthusiastic concubine. She would have preferred a society in which all males were from birth literally the slaves of women, and she would have treated her own slaves with a fine consideration.

On that April afternoon Beryl was evidently in acute distress, but as I had not seen her for almost a year (and was therefore not close to her mind) I hesitated to ask her point-blank to tell me what was amiss. After a silence that lasted a minute she looked up at me and said, "What do you guess?"

"Is Bob getting excited about somebody else?"

"A girl at the office."

"Which? Iron Supplies?"

"She's the General Manager's secretary, half Russian, and younger than I am."

I reminded Beryl that this was the oldest situation in the long story of mankind. "That doesn't help," she answered, "it's new to me." We cannot say anything fruitful when we are confronted by such woe unless we feel our way very carefully into the temperament of the sad one. As a rule, for example, "the wife," being either angry or miserable, becomes increasingly unattractive to "the man," while the paramour can easily be light-hearted, heart-easing, wantonly sex-lovely as any flower is, and even, sometimes, half-sorry for her dis-crowned rival. "Most wives," I suggested, "imagine that if they look dismal enough, their husbands will perceive how delicious and how magnetic they are and will instantly throw over the trumpery little creature who has inexplicably bemused an otherwise excellent citizen. . . ."

"I don't think Natalie *is* trumpery," interjected Beryl, "she's got brains as well as looks."

"Well," I continued, "how much do you think you can manage by way of self-discipline? You see, I have known just a few wives who, coming to this milestone in marriage, con-trived with some heroism to wear what we might call a Smiling Mask. In the first place, they don't let the new love hold all the court cards; and in the second, they not only make the man somewhat despise himself, but they take the gilt off that very adultery for which the husband has risked so much."

"I couldn't play-act," said Beryl.

"Of course," I admitted, "men ought to be monogamous, I know that: but no matter what fugues and fantasies we civilised persons may devise round it, sex in itself is a very simple tune. Life is passionately determined not to expire, and in that process it may use the shepherd only for two or three minutes (if he is a simple soul) but it must use the nymph for the best part of a year. Now, what is the shepherd, in a natural state of society, to do while the nymph contentedly nourishes the new little nymph or new little shepherd inside her body? Isn't it highly artificial to make such a to-do because the shepherd has dallied with a wandering dryad?"

Beryl frowned. "Bob's not a youngster! He ought to respect my dignity."

After a pause, I said, "Listen. This Natalie may be a loath-some girl, but suppose you give me a chance of seeing whether I can influence her at all? Suppose you tell Bob that you've been here. . . ."

"Yes?"

"And ask him to bring Natalie to dinner with me. I'll soon know if I can help."

"You men are so easily taken in."

I had heard this phrase so many times that, being jarred, I observed tartly, "Yes. You see, every woman is persuaded that she is the only decent and honourable woman in the world. It can hardly be true of every one, can it?"

III

Beryl used my suggestion, and I can only suppose that Bob agreed to it because the tension between them was becoming unbearable. Normally he would never have permitted me or anyone to inspect (as it were) his personal life. Perhaps he was hoping that I would report well of Natalie and miraculously reconcile Beryl to the whole affair.

They came to dinner, I notice, on April the 20th, and no sooner had my black-spectacled housekeeper grimly announced them (she owned a remarkable nose for sin) than I saw that Natalie had a distinguished and exotic charm. She resembled the elegant and sophisticated girl in Beardsley's beautiful drawing, "L'Éducation Sentimentale," and I felt certain that she must be the most dangerous Private Secretary in London. She had also high spirits and many delightful enthusiasms. Bob, as might be expected, began nervously, kept looking with bright-eyed admiration at his lovely captive and, moving to the sideboard, helped himself lavishly to some pre-dinner whiskies. To my surprise Natalie throughout the evening drank only water.

It was not until after dinner that, returning to the big room, we felt sufficiently at ease to discuss the cause of our meeting. Natalie, I observed, smoked only Turkish cigarettes and these in moderation. She had excited my imagination far more than I had expected, and I had already found out that she had no sense of sin and, rather more uncommonly, no desire for marriage. This I thought might possibly alleviate the trouble, for at least Bob would not need to go through that painful and undignified scene in which a man asks an unwilling wife to release him. Beryl could at least maintain her status.

"How is it all going to end?" I asked. "Even if Natalie doesn't mind sharing you, it's quite certain that Beryl does. And—in due time—Natalie may!"

"I don't think so," she said, with a sweet and confident smile. "I don't hate women. I like them. In fact, I believe I should like Beryl very much, if I had the chance!"

"It's all so damned ridiculous," ejaculated Bob. "Why shouldn't I love two entirely different women? You might as well say that if I like roses I'm not allowed to like arum-lilies. Besides, you've seen Natalie. You know she's not a rotter. Well, there it is—they're both fine people, and for the life of me I don't see why we can't be friends, the three of us."

"I suppose that's out of the question?" said Natalie.

"I've known it to be tried," I answered, "but I've never known it to succeed."

We were silent for a minute or two. I realised that Bob was far too deeply enamoured to be capable of renouncing Natalie. You might as well advise a man to keep cool in the Sahara. And Natalie had no conventional morality to which I could appeal. She simply could not understand what all the fuss was about: and when I observed, "But suppose you were in Beryl's place?" she replied, "It wouldn't make any difference. I'm not possessive and I don't mean to be possessed. All *that's* so primitive—like war-dances and witch-doctoring and totem worship. Surely you think so?"

"Bob!" I said, ominously, "what are you going to feel if Natalie claims her right to a second lover?"

"We've talked it out," he answered. "Everything would depend on the man's personality."

We were not getting any further, and although—as usual on such occasions—we stumbled round and round in a maze, we were quite unable to find our way out of it; and eventually, each of us a little tired of wandering aimlessly, we talked of other and easier topics—life in the F.M.S., the future of European women, the Soviet experiment, and whether it were better to be ruled by West End club-men or by Trades Union leaders.

Just as they were going, out there in the dark little entrance passage I said to Natalie, "And will you ever want children?"

She answered, "No. Not in an age like this. I'm just a bit too civilised, and I hope you think so!"

"Well, Bob," I sighed, "count on me to do what I can, though it's not much good for me to praise your Natalie. Beryl realises how easily I am taken in. . . ."

IV

Beryl would, of course, be anxious to know what had happened. So I rang her up immediately, while Bob Philipsway would still be driving Natalie home to her Bayswater flat. "She took me in completely," I said, "just as you said she would." "No, but what do you really think?" cried Beryl. "She is a new type. It may become general, especially if there's another world upheaval. She is genuinely unpossessive; and of course she can no more understand why you are possessive than she could understand if you wore a nose-ring."

Beryl was silent. I wondered what might be happening at the other end of the telephone. Presently she sobbed, "I'm coming to see you. At once. Good-bye." And she rang off.

I must admit that for a moment I thought fondly of my bed and wished that I had remained silent until the next morning. It was obvious that I had let myself in for a long and painful interview, but after all we are poor fellow-creatures if we do not give what help we may to those who are suffering the fantastic self-torments of "love." I lit a pipe and started the radio, and was lucky enough to stroll in upon the middle of a Sibelius symphony. My unhappy friend arrived a few minutes before twelve, and the next two hours were among the most distressing which I had experienced for perhaps a dozen years. Indeed, I have no intention of describing Beryl's misery in detail. She cried recklessly, and it was some time before any words emitted by my mind made any impression at all upon her mind: but inevitably her woe attained its crisis and was followed by a sort of desolate calm. I had seen San Francisco two days after the earthquake had shattered it. Over the city spread a rust-brown awning of smoke, and a few fires were still burning; nor can there ever have been so deep a stillness in San Francisco, day or night.

I said to Beryl, partly in order to lure her away from herself, "I was always a romantic. I have lived into a superficial era which regards romance as either childish or much too dangerous; but, you see, it does mean that I have some experience of ecstasy and of despair. . . ."

"I've always known that about you," she said, trying to check her tears.

"So don't think me inhuman, like a lawyer," I went on, "if I ask you three or four questions. You may not have found out why you are so wretched. . . ."

Then I asked her if the cause of so much pain was a crude sexual-possessiveness, and she thought that this was not so. Was she afraid lest Natalie would supplant her as Bob's wife? She understood that they had no wish to marry. Well, then, could it all come from injured self-respect—the feeling that Bob ought not to have found anybody more attractive, at least for a while, than she herself was? Oh, yes—that came into it, no doubt. And finally I suggested, quite without foreseeing my very next move, that the main cause of her wild grief was probably the knowledge that henceforth there would be a big section of Bob's life and interest and hope and happiness in which she could not have any part. Here—it seemed—I had struck the truth, for again she broke down, saying incoherently that the old harmony was ruined for ever, that she did not want to be merely his half-time companion, that as she had not the strength of character to let him go—go "to that woman"— the only sensible action was to put herself out of the way for good and all. She got up and stood with her back to me, looking sightlessly at the contents of my principal bookcase.

"D'you suppose," I ventured, "that there's anybody in the whole of London who has never considered committing suicide? Let me assure you that when a few years have gone by, we are mighty pleased that we had not had quite the nerve to bring it off."

She swerved round. "What else can I do, what else? Tell me!"

Suddenly my voice replied, "Meet her. Come to dinner here. I'll invite Natalie and a man-friend—Eric Gillett, perhaps."

When I heard these words I expected a burst of anger, but Beryl was silent; and, a little desperately, I added, "You love high-finish in painting or literature. You will find it in this young woman. And at the very least, wouldn't it be better to see her for yourself before—well, before saying good-bye to everything? You'd have more to think about in the next world."

It must have been two o'clock when we went down the Rope Walk and when the night porter fetched a taxi from the Piccadilly rank.

V

It was early in May that I managed to contrive my little dinner-party. The emotional potentialities of the evening were so dangerous and impredictable that I had chosen Eric Gillett as my table-opposite, knowing that, even although I could tell him nothing about the situation, he would tack skilfully if we encountered any head-winds. It seemed best, moreover, to make sure that he should be the first arrival. The presence of a stranger would allow the women, while carrying on a light conversation with him, to become a little used to one another.

Moreover, Eric had lived for some years in Singapore and so, when Beryl arrived, they had no difficulty in breaking the ice. True, he had never met the Philipsways, but they and he had a good many mutual friends, and Beryl seemed happy to talk about a country and a period in which her life had seemed set for a fair course to the end. I, meanwhile, hovering on the edge of their Malayan reminiscences, awaited with some trepidation the faint noise of the front-door bell. I did not expect a Billingsgate scene, but I was half afraid that we should hear at least a few venomous overtones and that Beryl might invent or develop a headache which would take her home early. Were these women sufficiently civilised as to give this hazardous experiment any chance of doing good?

As Natalie arrived (she looked more exotic than ever in her flame-coloured cloak and her golden sandals). Eric was in the midst of an amusing tale, and for some seconds Beryl did not realise that my new guest was in the room with her. I led

Natalie to the sideboard where the drinks were marshalled, doing so in order that Beryl might have a few moments in which to appraise her. Then, relying on Eric to keep the merriment alive at least upon the surface, I effected the introductions. Beryl's expression was enigmatic. It certainly contained admiration. Natalie showed a frank and happy surprise. Nevertheless, it was just as well that Eric should have occupied us just then by speaking of a large and bibulous major who frequented one of the hotel bars in Singapore. Two very small Colonels were, it seemed, perched on high stools at this bar, sipping their stingahs, when—to the horror of everyone except Eric—the Major strolled along, knocked the heads of the Colonels together, and called out, "Fight, you little devils, fight!"

Soon afterwards dour Miss Fraser announced dinner, and we went upstairs. Eric continued to talk in his most charming and varied manner, so that the time passed with surprising rapidity; and occasionally I engaged Eric in male conversation —about cricket, for instance—precisely in order that with my mind's ear I might catch the notes of that other and more difficult conversation which ran across ours. To my relief and uncertain delight Beryl and Natalie seemed actually to be getting on together with no apparent strain. What is more, when dinner was over and they decided to repair their faces, they went together into the little bathroom, seeming to stay there for a propitious length of time. It was all very puzzling, and I wished again and again that I were free to take Eric into Beryl's confidence.

And so, in fact, did the whole of that memorable evening go by, the two women opening out, at first cautiously, and then more and more like flowers in a sunny midday, until I should have supposed if I had not known the trouble of the last few weeks that I had effected a new and cordial friendship. Late in the evening, under some pretext, I took Beryl to a corner of the room, almost whispering, "Well?" And she answered, "*What* a beauty!"

My surprise touched its apex, however, when the party was ending. Eric offered to take a taxi and see the two ladies home.

Natalie said that she had brought her car (a Morris Eight), and offered to give Eric a lift, but he found that she lived in the opposite direction from his own. "Then I'll come along," I said, "and get a taxi for Mrs. Philipsway." "You certainly won't!" cried Natalie, "we've arranged all that. She's coming with *me*."

About ten minutes later, Eric was in the hall, tying his evening scarf. "I've never watched two of them before," he observed. "What do you mean?" I asked. "Ah," he said, chuckling mysteriously, "and is Philipsway happy about it?" Before I could find out how much he had divined, my friend was down the stone stairs on his way to that literary eyrie in Earl's Court Square.

VI

For the next few weeks I seem to have been out of touch with Natalie and the Philipsways. Towards the end of June an entirely altered Beryl did have the grace to say down the telephone, "It's all too marvellous. How did you guess?" But when I petitioned for more light, she merely said laughingly, "Ask Bob. You've made both of us *so* happy!" Then, provocatively, she rang off.

More mystified than ever, I did write a note to Philipsway, and he rang up, that evening. Among the other phrases which I heard with gathering wonder were, "Natalie's living with us now . . . I never thought it possible, but, you see, the Eternal Triangle has proved to be equilateral. . . . Yes, I do mean that. Isn't it better to have two lovers than just one, and if there are three persons each can have two lovers. Q.E.D. You must come and give our *ménage* your blessing. . . ."

I was due to dine that evening with Leon M. Lion at the Ivy. In the course of our happy and easy interchange I told him the foregoing story, using then, as now, fictitious names. His eyebrows lifted; his eyeglass dropped; his face puckered into a tolerant smile which would have done credit to Lao-tze; and he observed, quoting Montaigne, "How *un*dulant and *di*verse is human nature—mmm?"

XII

THE BURLINGTON BOMB

AS I sat writing at my table one morning a squall of un-easiness went over me. I walked to the window and looked down, as on so many happier occasions, at the newspaper-man who stood at the junction of Vigo Street and Savile Row. The two words which he was displaying caused me to sweat throughout the morning. They were:

POLAND

INVADED

They foretold unimaginable misery. They signified that all Europe, or so I imagined, would be maimed and impoverished by another world-rocking war; that great or lovely and ancient cities would be insanely shattered; and that innumerable fine works of art, engineering and maternity would be smashed and wasted. My thoughts flew across Europe to a noble-hearted and highly cultured lady who lived in Cracow, to Helena Myslakowska, who, only a year earlier, had sat on the very couch that I could still see, telling me much about her country.

When Poland had been sandbagged there was, as everybody knows, a long mysterious lull. Americans, perhaps a little disappointed by so much mere clinching, told us that this was a "phoney war." It was certainly a war which during the winter of 1939 had almost no effect upon life in Albany. Presently, it is true, the East End of London experienced that diabolical bomb-dropping from the black sky which all of us had been anticipating for some months; but for a long while the West End remained almost immune—not without astonishment.

After some months of brick-like welsh-rabbit I saw the last of Mrs. Freitag, and replaced her with Amaryllis, a twenty-year-old housekeeper, dark, trim, pretty, and minute. At this time I had gradually acquired the attic-floor of the G block. It contained a very small but exceedingly desirable flat which had been rendered almost luxurious by an American gentleman. He had gone home, and the "gingerbread flat," as we called it, was now occupied, much to my gratification, by Julian and Margery Herbage. Miss Morris, the American play-producer, had a small room on that floor, and the colony was completed, as it were, by Amaryllis, who had the room opposite. And so during the early weeks of 1940 we lived in peace and amity, but

> Alas, regardless of their doom,
> The little victims play!
> No sense have they of ills to come,
> Nor care beyond to-day,

and how prophetically the poet continues!

> Yet see how all around 'em wait
> The Ministers of human fate,
> And black Misfortune's baleful train!
> Ah, shew them where in ambush stand
> To seize their prey the murth'rous band!

II

The "murth'rous band" was still at this period preoccupied with crushing the French and with massacring the inoffensive Dutch; but from the early days of that summer we Londoners became more and more accustomed to the lamentable cater-wauling of the ill-named "sirens," but it was not until France was raped, prone, and powerless, not until autumn began to darken our evenings, that the enemy seriously set about to batter old London into submission. Spruce Captain Adams, the debonair Secretary of Albany, had long since contrived a commodious air-raid shelter, and thither on three or four occasions, passing along the cold and ancient cellars from our end to his end of Albany, Amaryllis and I repaired. She was a brave little creature, however, and before long we decided to remain at "home" and in comfort unless London's anti-aircraft gunfire became ominously loud and continuous.

We had not to wait long. At ten o'clock on an evening in September the loud-wailer keened wildly from the roof of Savile Row police-station. Down in the dark street foot-steps quickened. An air-raid warden shouted something to a colleague. After a few moments somebody knocked at the door of the flat. Then Amaryllis came in, announcing, "Miss Morris and Mr. Coburn."

"Just a moment," I said. "Amaryllis, I don't much like the sound of this raid. Probably nothing will happen, but I'd like you to sleep on the couch upstairs in the dining-room."

"All right," she answered, with characteristic imperturbability.

Then Marjorie Morris said, apologetically, "Max and I have a lot of theatre business to talk over. If the bombs get really close, may we come down here for a while?"

Towards midnight the raid became savage. Our part of London was bellowing and bull-roaring all round us, and once or twice I thought I could distinguish the fuller and more self-satisfied detonation of a high-explosive bomb. I was relieved and not surprised when Max and Marjorie reappeared at my door, though all of us knew that two upper storeys of an antique building would give us no protection against a direct hit. The ferocity of the cannonade had awakened Amaryllis, who, clad in a nightgown, an overwrap, and little puffed bed-shoes, came gliding through the doorway with a well furnished tea-tray.

I have never been quite so much in two minds. Since I was responsible for these three souls, ought I to steer them along the dark vaults and into Captain Adams' raid-shelter at the Piccadilly end? Was it folly to remain in my rooms with so many big guns booming about us, or would it be merely lily-livered if we racked our limbs, hour after hour, upon the exiguous deck-chairs in that sepulchral shelter? It seemed so unlikely that bombs dropped from a height of perhaps two miles, and having a target of some twenty thousand buildings, should crash precisely upon our little outpost of Albany, that I thought, "Here we have tea, whisky, limitless tobacco, and comfortable chairs. We may as well risk it"; and I said to Amaryllis, "What do you want to do? I suggest that you go upstairs again, and get a good night's sleep."

"All right," she replied, as always, and I expect that she obediently slept. "You know," I said, turning to the others, "if I were to say to that child, 'Go down to Somerset this afternoon and bring back a lemon-coloured hollyhock, she would answer, 'All right,' and fulfil her mission."

Miss Morris, rolled up in blankets and eiderdowns (for no American has ever had a good circulation), fell asleep on the old green couch. Max Coburn, cocooned in the residue of my blanket-store, curled up on the carpet. And going into my room, which was next door, I shed my clothes to a fearsome accompaniment of anti-aircraft gunfire, donned pyjamas and an old dressing-gown, and lay down, not at all confidently, on top of my bedclothes. I still wondered what I ought to do with those three souls. I risked it again.

Responsibility kept me awake. All that I could do was to remember my youthful practice of yoga, stilling my thoughts as best I could and reminding myself that death is a condition of being born and is, in all conscience, common enough. "Almost hackneyed," I thought, "and we must find some new 'curtain' for our tragic dramas. . . . Wedding-bells, prophesying woe, now give an ironical end to a comedy; and if death is only a liberation of the soul, it even gives to our tragedies a happy and lovely close! If death is freedom, it is no tragic finale, and if marriage is imprisonment. . . . At this moment I heard a gigantic tailor suddenly ripping two miles of calico. London shrieked. The German high-explosive bomb, bursting at the north end of Burlington Arcade—about seventy yards away—made a vaster noise than any which I had supposed to be producible. That bomb had instantly demolished five shops.

I jumped up. I thought distinctly that another bomb was not likely to fall any closer. What are seventy yards to an aeroplane? I fumbled for my torch, and went on to the landing. Amaryllis, like some precocious little student in the part of Lady Macbeth, was walking downstairs to the fragile safety of the first floor. She was so sleepy that she came down barefoot. "Let's see how they've stood it," I said.

To my amazement neither Marjorie nor Max was more than dimly awake. They mumbled and then turned over. "You'd better go back to bed," I told Amaryllis, "nothing worse will happen now." "All right," she said, and returned to the couch in the dining-room.

I wondered what damage that bomb had done: but the guns were still pounding away, and I dared not make much use of a torch. I had, in fact, to feel my way round the rooms: it was obvious that most of the windows had been shattered and that some of the window-frames were sticking inward at odd uncanny angles, like dislocated fingers.

"Pretty bad," I thought, "but I shall not be able to see what has really happened till dawn comes"; and, passing the peaceful figures of Max and Marjorie, I went back to my room and lay upon the bed. And I thought, "So that's the noise of a heavy bomb, is it? How odd, and how woeful, and how incomprehensible it is that one kind of man should wish to drop explosives on another kind of man. . . . But I do wish daylight would come. I want to see what's happened."

As soon as daylight did come, I explored the flat. Not much of the glass was left. Then I went on to the balcony in the cold grey dawn. Steel-hatted policemen were there at the junction of Savile Row and Vigo Street. Busy midgets were sweeping up masses of shattered glass; and I noticed that Vigo Street had been roped off, but (in those early days) I did not appreciate the meaning of that fact. I dressed. I went out. I saw that "my" end of the Arcade was a Pompeian ruin. Dainty shoes and bright jewellery were scattered upon the pavement. I went back. Amaryllis was now awake, was preparing our breakfasts; and in due time Max and Marjorie, those drowsy effigies, opened their eyes and vaguely recollected that something a little out of the ordinary had happened.

After breakfast they went away, nor shall I ever know how far, if at all, they were conscious of having endured a terrific minute or two in that Battle of London which will never be forgotten. In future, when such scientific violence is no longer imaginable, many historians not yet born and not within a generation of being born, will attempt vainly to describe that first, ferocious and atavistic onslaught upon the huge old heart of England. As for me, I went once more on to the balcony in order to view the scene. Even now it was, I suppose, not

8

later than eight-fifteen. How strange, I mused, to see this wild damage in a part of London which is so densely ivied with memories of the leisured, the well-to-do, and the so-called 'naughty' 'nineties. . . ."

At this moment a genial steel-hatted policeman caught sight of me. "You can't stay here," he announced.

"I am an Englishman," I retorted, "and until my lease expires, this is my castle!"

"Can't help that," said he. "Police orders. You must move out. There's an unexploded land-mine," he confided, "over there in Regent Street, forty yards from your window."

Taking Amaryllis under my wing, I went to stay with a friend in the country. A week later, the mine having been neutralised, I returned; but on the very next night the bombardment which carved a broad slice out of Savile Row was so furious that Amaryllis and I were glad that we had sought refuge in the Albany shelter. The Savile Row bombs, half a dozen in half a minute, completed the wreckage of my windows, and once more I went with Amaryllis to that welcoming friend in the country.

Within a week or ten days an incendiary bomb alighted unnoticed upon the top of the G block and, left to itself, burned joyously for five or six hours before the resulting illumination attracted the attention of an intelligent passer-by. Already, however, that fire-bomb had completely burnt away the top floor of the block—the gingerbread flat, and Marjorie Morris's little room, and the other little room which was full of Amaryllis's photographs, nick-nacks, dresses, and silk stockings. Firemen arrived and shot water on to the smouldering block for something like forty-eight hours, utterly ruining all my carpets, most of my household linen, and much of my Sheraton furniture. Indeed, when—summoned by telephone —we arrived at that ruin, bent upon rescuing with all speed the books, the furniture, my pictures and my clothes, the acid hose-water lay ankle-deep on the old uneven floor of the flat.

And in the course of superintending that sad evacuation, I went on to the landing outside what had been for so long my front-door. I saw Margery Herbage coming downstairs—very much like a Renaissance angel from heaven, for above the stairs there was no longer any ceiling. "I've been to the gingerbread flat," she said. "Of course, it's all gone, and everything's burnt, including Julian's London clothes; but I did find these —look—some of the old family silver!"

III

That bomb had crashed into the elegant world of the 'nineties. I could see without difficulty the disgust of a dozen dandified ghosts. How well they had known Savile Row, Burlington Gardens, and the Bodley Head, which actually underpropped my rooms—how much they had relished this corner of London, Aubrey Beardsley, Oscar Wilde, Eugene Lee-Hamilton, Dowson, Davidson, and that old ne'er-do-well the Baron Carvo and, in fact, all those who had made The Yellow Book an intellectual aphrodisiac which has had no equal, before or since, with the exception of Petronius Arbiter's glittering romance. Their Burlington Arcade, a notorious aviary in the exquisite 'nineties, had been damaged to an extent not conceivable by those happy dilettanti. Even if, jingling past in their spectral hansoms, they glanced at the Bodley Head, the bow-windowed room above it and the smoking remnant of the gingerbread flat, they presumed, I suppose, that London had been shaken by a too-too delightful earthquake.

IV

The same little bomb had ended for me a happy, September-ish, soft-golden phase of a life which I had never imagined would last into the 'fifties. And, remembering how instantaneous death had missed me and my guests by much less than a hundred yards, I fell into a pleasingly melancholic mood. I recalled, for example, how a doctor had once told me that hardly anybody is aware of dying and that, as a rule, the moment which may have been dreaded throughout a long lifetime, as it was by Dr. Johnson, comes and goes, after all, unnoticed. Even if this were not true, how many persons, I wondered, would feel a wild regret in saying farewell to this world? For myself, I agreed with Tess of the d'Urbervilles that "ours is one of the blighted stars," but I was also prepared to maintain that there can be no worlds which are not blighted. Humanity, it is true, has added immeasurable disgrace to the record of this planet but, underlying all the violence of humanity, there is that fundamental ferocity of Nature which would in itself have been enough to make the heart sick.

Then, I thought, yes, what you say is quite true, but the mechanism of Nature, seemingly devised by an Imagination which is indifferent to suffering and cruelty, stands in puzzling contrast to all the undeniable beauty which was presumably invented by the same artificer. Perhaps the life-lover is not keenly aware of the world's pain but, on the other hand, it is possible to be so obsessed by a recognition of pain that we are not fair to God and give him no credit for his attempts to charm us. Is not this over-occupation with pain the defect in Buddhism?

Even those of us who feel, with the witty undergraduate, that "life is very much over-rated" and who hear with astonishment about "God's love and mercy," can certainly remember a fair share of happiness: and at this I began to wonder how my friends would answer the question "Now that you have died, what experiences in the old life are you sorry to have left for ever?" Unfortunately I was alone, and in consequence could hear none but my own answers.

There was no doubt of it, I should have to include experiences of "love," even although "the sea's caresses" are "kinder than love's that betrays and blesses": and of course I should put near the top of my list that sharing of hopes, ambitions, ideas, tribulations and delights which constitutes friendship. I should also remember the Sussex downs at twilight, and orchards of Somerset whether in blossom or fruit, and all Tudor buildings from Compton Wynyates or Penshurst Palace to any thatched farmhouse or cottage that was built in the golden days. That made me think upon music, and how much it had consoled or encouraged or kindled me. . . . Nearly all nineteenth-century Russian music, I thought, and yet chiefly Tchaikovski and Rimsky-Korsakov: but indeed my obligation to music was so deep that I could hardly get beyond a consideration of it, because, after all, much as the world-composers had given to me, I had still to confess that old English music from Byrd to Purcell—gallant in gaiety or sorrow—had perhaps created the subtlest and profoundest of all my happy memories. My delight in "Greensleeves," for instance, became a joke against me among my friends.

Italian cities and the old warm landscapes of Tuscany: Girgenti, Taormina, almost every square yard of Sicily: and the bay of Naples at night—these also had meant much to me; and because they were far away, infinitely far away by reason of war, association carried me out to sea, and I was again voyaging in a noble and powerful liner, and there, in mid-Atlantic or mid-Pacific, looked out on the almost slumbering ocean and at the moon and the enigmatical stars. Why are they there? I mused; what is the use of those gigantic globes of metal and gas? Did they get there by themselves, and how long have they been gyrating through the inspissated blackness of space?

I was getting out of my depth, for Astronomy can easily start a panic in the mind; and with an unpremeditated chuckle I thought again of Commander C. B. Fry. He had chatted with Hitler, and was not Fry a man who, like Romeo, would "defy the stars"? Rising by a mere semitone of memory, I now re-experienced all the passionate pleasure which I had once derived from games—from hockey, tennis, lawn-tennis, croquet, squash-rackets, and cricket; and I realised that when the hour came I also might babble o' green fields, for I might well be thinking of Lords, the Oval, Horsham, Canterbury, or of many a pretty village ground in the West Country whereon I had played so buoyantly in my youth. I hoped that there would be test matches in heaven and that Fry, getting there first, would make sure of a grandstand box. I knew that he would invite me to that box and I found myself questioning whether the champagne and caviare of heaven could possibly be more delicious than their earthly counterparts had been. . . .

By this time I was in a mood for metaphysics, and my veteran cherrywood was therefore recalled for duty.

Deciding to put my hopes and convictions on parade so that

I might inspect them, I knew that for me psychical research had conclusively demonstrated, however surprising the fact may be, that the mind does not perish with the body; and, having thus restored the soul to its bygone dignity, I could not see why anybody should be unable to accept the ancient "theory" of reincarnation. On the contrary, if we conclude that spirit and matter are entirely different forces which, nevertheless, can, as we know, unite, then reincarnation provides the simplest conceivable mechanism for effecting that union. Spirit, I reflected, is probably akin to light—that strangest of all mysteries— continually assaulting the physical world and being refracted by physical objects into ten thousand varying hues. In my fancy I could see quite clearly how spirit becomes entangled in matter and cannot get out of it, and how it keeps on returning or being pulled back again as new bodies are formed for entrapping it. At this moment, in fact, I pictured the world of bodies as a fountain which never ceased to play because each gallon of water when it fell or died went back to the reservoir and in due time shot up again into the air.

But people, I argued against myself, maintain that if we have lived before, we should remember what we have done, and they also declare that it is impossible to conceive of spirit without form. Come now, O mind musing inside that silvering head, what do you say to these objections? Why, firstly, that I cannot remember anything even of my present life during the first eight years of it, and yet the events of those years are said to have been more formative than any subsequent experiences: and so my past lives may certainly have shaped my so-called personality even although I have forgotten every detail of every life. Or have I not quite forgotten? Why does Tudor music affect me as definitely as the strong soft fragrance of syringa? And do I not share with a multitude of Europeans, alive now or living within the last six centuries, an unaccountable nostalgia for the life of ancient Greece? Perhaps we think most kindly of the times and places in which we led our happiest lives, for to do so would be only an enlargement of what we feel as we review the many phases of our current life. Why did I speak of syringa? Now I come to consider it, I did so precisely because

I was an exceedingly happy youth on a certain evening when I first smelt that fragrance.

Well, said my Intellectual Conscience, that may be so—just possibly—but you have not answered my other crux. How can spirit exist without form?

Even after death, I replied to myself, spirit may not be without form. You know well enough what you mean when you say that a musical work has form: but obviously a musical form is not visible and has no corporeality. Perhaps—who knows? —the disembodied spirit has a time-form instead of a form in space? Or at least, as in music and poetry, a form predominantly temporal, and as for "space," is it not one of our basic mysteries, and may there not be many kinds of space?

Anyway, the point is (I continued) that psychical research has convinced me that personality remains intact after death for quite a fair number of years, and I feel no more called upon to explain how it can do so than to account for the existence of the sun.

I was now well away and ascending into the stratosphere, and it was almost natural that I should consider again that curious and brilliant notion that just as my little finger is a fragment of my body so may my soul be merely a fragment of a group-soul—itself one of many vast, magnificent, and fundamental spirits who again, like intermediate colours, may ultimately derive from "the Lord's Seven Spirits who shine through the rain" and so create a rainbow round the throne of the Innermost.

Supposing, then, that each of us is only a cell of more or of less importance within a mighty spiritual entity, then we should understand how in one life I may have to suffer for some disharmony which you—and not I—set up in a life long ago! If our group-soul is not feeling well, I as its big-toe-joint may have to suffer because you, as its tongue, drank too much pleasure. Yes, I reflected, that is a possibility which greatly enriches the doctrine of Karma. . . . And if reincarnation is a fact—if Karma, or a mechanical tendency in the universe to keep balanced, is also a fact—then what an incentive we have—beyond the stretch of H. G. Wells's mind—to see that the conditions of our world shall improve! We shall inherit the world which we make.

Still dreaming in this wantonly unscientific spirit, I fell to wondering whether perhaps I might next be born in a feminine body, nor did the possibility alarm me; only, I did perceive how important it is for us men, while we have some time in hand, to improve the status of women. But then a cold horror swept over my imagination. I foresaw the cruel possibility that Fate, in order to bevel away my prejudices, might steer me, as I came drifting downwards from the innermost paradise of Devachan, into a French household; and, scraping out my English cherry-wood, I vowed in self-defence to cultivate, if possible, a love for the French people.

   .   .   .   .   .

A few days ago I went to London, to battered, wounded, heroic London, and my business took me past the Vigo Street end of Albany. I looked up. That bedroom window, desolately open, had little glass left in it. The high bow-window, on the farther side of which I had worked so happily for eight years, still carried most of the criss-cross paper which I had put up there on the day when Poland was invaded; and on my derelict balcony the peace-time creepers were still creeping, indifferent to the presence in their world of Homo Sapiens: but a new phase of life had been forced upon me and, turning away, I recognised that humanity was rapidly advancing, in its blind manner, towards a new phase of social life.

XIII
CAMBRIDGE UNTOUCHABLES

1

IT was now necessary to find a new hut, roof-tree, or igloo. I cannot write the words "a new home" because for me there can be no home except London or Nirvana. However, I was lucky in my igloo. "This," said Viola Garvin at one of Lion's gay dinner-parties, "is a good war: it is making people kind to each other"; and at least for the first two years her saying was true.

For instance, throughout the perilous autumn of 1940 I found harbourage, as Amaryllis did, with that friend—equally wise and warm-hearted—who lived in an olden farmhouse which lay many winding and leafy miles from a station; and here, although bombs from German factories churned up the mild Essex fields, rattled our windows at night and cracked those Henry the Seventh walls of "wattle and daub"—here, nevertheless, we survived.

And then, in the smallest hours of a November morning, I remembered some bygone visits to Cambridge, a town some twenty miles away as the car flies; and at once I thought of Dr. Philip Gosse, the pirate-fancier; of Professor Ifor Evans, already an evacuee howsoever august; and of the composer, Patrick Hadley, a curly-headed Cambridge aboriginal who was reputed to know every water-hole in the district. My unruly loves and hates in literature might, I surmised, be clipped and groomed by Professor Evans; my simple and savage enthusiasms in music would, I believed, be tactfully fostered or refined by Dr. Hadley; and I trusted that Dr. Gosse, who also had not graduated in any university, would give me his moral support if, like him, I were to seek exile in a little town so charming and so famous.

And what, in fact, was I remembering about Cambridge? I found myself sniffing a delightful nosegay of emotions. Had I been more docile at the age of eighteen I should have come as an undergraduate to King's College, almost simultaneously with Rupert Brooke: and despite the little puffs and squalls of literary fashion, that, in my opinion, would have been a memorable experience. I was even remembering how, by a fluke of friendship, I had stood in the nave of King's Chapel at almost the very time when I might have stood there as the freshest of Freshmen, and had been deliciously overwhelmed by such high beauty of carven stone and coloured glass, thinking that this airy building looked less like a Christian chapel than a palace which Merlin or Prospero had invoked by enchantment and had forgotten to dissolve. Well, if I settled in

Cambridge I should certainly be something of a Prodigal Son, but I still wondered whether a great University, though tolerating much variegation and oddity of mind, would have welcomed a young man who read Davydd ap Gwilym with delight but Livy with loathing, who was already experimenting with raja-yoga and fairly familiar with the Upanishads and Patanjali, and who was redeemed from utter eccentricity only by an inordinate enthusiasm for cricket.

It was, indeed, cricket which next brought me back. A formidable team of analytical chemists from London University, led by Hugh Prew (an Englishman to be proud of), had challenged the Vacation Elevens, an innocent, unsuspecting tribe of fuzzy-wuzzies who stood up cheerfully but in vain to the maxim-gun bowling of our captain. There had been, I recalled, a gay match on the St. John's College ground; but now, gazing from the wrong side of the railings, I often recall how

> a Peri at the gate
> Of Eden stood, disconsolate.

And in the end, too, I was thinking of an evening when, after talking about the National Theatre, I had gone soberly to sleep at the Bull Inn, only to be awakened at two in the morning by a repeated upheaval of myself and my bed, as though some Caliban had lain slumbering beneath me and was now uneasily turning. This was the night of that earthquake which, presumably, had lost its way in the dark.

I walked happily into the office of a sleek and bald-headed house-agent, but he said nothing, lifted his eyebrows and suggested the door. A second agent, slightly more humane, chuckled "You don't understand. People are scrambling for the very stables of Cambridge." A third agent had settled my fate within two or three days, and what is more, had done handsomely.

II

The practice of any art is best followed in youth, and the world would be a more joyous planet if most writers would close their shops when they had been living for forty-five years: and I, like any superannuated Colonel or rheumatical farmer, had meant to retire and to loll away the rest of my time, not without dignity, at Lord's or Wimbledon, in the cultivation of friendships or the contemplation of beauty. The second German War, however, had bombed me to Cambridge, and I was not too certain how the natives would receive yet one more slum-child from London, seeing that some twenty-five thousand had previously arrived.

Philip Gosse (an Old Boy, as it were) at once did his best to support me. He was already President of the South Sussex Stickleback Association, and he now proposed that we should found the Society of Cambridge Untouchables. You were an Untouchable if you had never studied at Oxford or Cambridge, at Harvard or Yale, membership of the other universities remaining *sub judice*. I elected Gosse as Founder-President, laying down the rule that in public he must always be referred to as "His Touchiness." Graduates might not attend more than two dinners a year, and even then were to pay an apologia of five shillings. Touch-typists were eligible for membership *ipso facto*; and so was any Welshman, on the assumption that he was touchy. The opening toast at any reunion of the Untouchables was to be a Health to Mr. Gandhi, drunk in water. Gosse wanted the Society's uniform to consist of a light-blue loincloth, but he withdrew the motion when I pointed out that under this provision the touch-typists might bring the whole venture into disrepute. All should have gone well with us, had not out Founder-President shamelessly quisling'd and gone over to the Doctors of Philosophy.

The natives, if they loathed us, dissimulated bravely. It is not merely that there are twenty-five thousand of us, but that all of us are fat, voluble, and unlovely. In addition we have four elbows apiece, eight or ten charmless children, and either two "prams" or three. The local omnibuses, again, were dreamily designed for short, lean scholars ("the sense of tall folk," said Hafiz, "has no fame") or for slender and irresistible Girtonians, not for beings of our bulk and altitude. And no sooner has the vehicle regurgitated us than we assemble in garrulous clots at those very points which, thus held, can most incommode the graceful, quiet, and well-educated natives.

They—in their official preserves at Peterhouse or Caius—
may be tired of the local antiquities. What Tasmanian can share
the anthropologist's excitement over the uncanny looping of
a boomerang? The true-black Tasmanian turns aside, and no
doubt the true-blue Cantabrigian smiles at our parvenu
raptures, our trite but happy reflections. And yet it is difficult
to live here without insensibly absorbing a history degree. It
is hard to believe that the architectural beauty of the colleges,
whether Georgian, Tudor, or Plantagenet, will leave no effect
upon the impressionable minds of young men or even upon our
own more obfuscated senses. They and we may not apprehend
all this beauty until life has huddled us away elsewhere, but all
of us will have seen what a building can be.

Again, I can never saunter between those towering limes of
Trinity Avenue, a majestic walk which was first laid out in
1672, without musing upon the myriads of Cambridge men who
have seen and admired them; and then I fall to speculating
whether these actual trees are old enough to have seen Wordsworth plain, and I decide that probably they just missed him;
but I feel fairly confident that as young-trees-about-town they
must have nodded to young Alfred Tennyson. And of course
I am comfortably certain that Rupert Brooke and they are very
old friends. Lovely they are, and most consolatory, no matter
what is the season of the year, because their quiet and dreaming
personalities continually impress upon us the ephemerality of
our current anxieties and woes. Throughout the slow years of
the last war they stood where they now stand, and throughout the Crimean War and the Indian Mutiny, and perhaps
even during the long-drawn nightmare of Napoleon's grandifi-
cence.

And then as I come out into narrow Trinity Lane with its
medieval walls and defensive windows, the bicycling errand-
boys and the mechanics of the R.A.F. eye me a little dubiously
if they catch me fingering some commonplace flint in the wall,
not knowing of course that I am wondering whether Kit
Marlowe may have given it a touch one day as he passed.
Even old Spenser must have seen that wall, and so must that
"base fellow and rogue" (as Jonson unkindly called him), that

exquisite poet, John Day of Caius. Such thoughts are themselves enough to send me home the happier, but on my way
home, if it is fine and dry, how pleasant to prolong my truancy
from the pen, and to paddle or punt for an hour or so on the
Chinese Cam or the stoutly British Granta. No—I must believe
that when we leave Cambridge we shall be less uncouth than
we are at present: nor can anyone dwell in this green and
flowery town without daily giving thanks to the king's, archi-
tects, poets, and scholars of olden time, or without a prayer that
Cambridge may inspire the men of the near future as she is now
inspiring and civilising us.

Last summer there was grievously little cricket, for the young
men were either cramming for examinations or drilling against
possible invasion: and that is probably why, sitting yesterday
beside the Cam with its weeping willows and amorous bridges,
I thought to myself, "What a team of poets this old town could
send into the field! Why, in her marvellous pedigree of poets
Cambridge excels all other towns from China to Peru!" Then,
warming to this test-match of my fancy, I became vainglorious
and told the listening air that, poet for poet, my First Eleven
could knock any Oxford team into an unrecognisable cocked
hat, and that even my Second Eleven was not to be sneezed at.

Why was not Charles Fry at my elbow, eager to say his best
for Oxford? In person he was far away but, hoping that he
might be present astrally, I addressed him as follows: "Charles,
you will admit that my opening pair, Milton and Wordsworth,
will take a deal of shifting, nor do I see how the wild fast
bowling of Shelley and Swinburne, your most dangerous pair,
could ever separate them. My number three is that dashing
amateur, milord Byron, and he in due course will be replaced
by a batsman no less redoubtable than Edmund Spenser who,
as the world knows, can remain at the wickets all day. . . .
When Milton has run out old Spenser, both being somewhat
slow on their pins, that noble stylist Alfred Tennyson comes
majestically down the pavilion steps: and what comfort will
there next be (for you and Oxford) in the sight of Dryden's
broad and sensible bat? Who would not flinch from the Jessop
of my team—Kit Marlowe with his mighty line? Think, too,

of my bowlers—old Robert Greene, a twister, John Day with his lobs, Rupert Brooke and, above all, Thomas Gray, who never loses his length. . . . Come, my dear man, admit frankly that in poetry Cambridge could challenge the whole world!"

III

The King and Queen of Cambridge have done much for the culture of the town. They offer us the best of music, drama, and ballet. King Maynard (whom Queen Lydia so quaintly calls "Keynes")[1] could not fail, I fancy, in any venture, and the Arts Theatre is well supported by many of the University students and by a few of us London waifs and strays. Masters, Fellows, and Dons apparently consider that the world has nothing more to give them, and in a Combination Room it may even be bad form to have attended a concert or a play. I believe that some of the Fellows have a clear conception of London as a large city in the West of England.

How should we fare, we simpler and more enthusiastic folk, if it were not for that patronage of the arts which comes so easily to Maynard Keynes and Lydia Lopokova? We might sink to the level of Brighton or Exeter or Bradford. Every social system has its defects, but it seems to be true that all the arts flourish best where there is a prince of taste and intelligence who gives his people no opportunity of revelling in vulgarity or trash.

XIV

SOME TALK OF ALEXANDER

I

NOTHING is more likely than that, when the world recovers a rationed share of leisure, a generation shall arise, perhaps in the nineteen-fifties, which will sentimentalise the fancied charm of the eighteen-sixties. Horse-hair and silken smoking-caps will be all the rage. Croquet may enjoy a fantastic revival, and there may well be an attempt (abortive, it is true) at

[1] These lines were written when he was still Mr. Keynes.

re-popularising whalebone and whiskers. That crusade will probably start in Oxford, and in Oxford be relegated to the celebrated scrapheap of lost causes.

The eighteen-sixties, let us bear in mind, were peaceful and, at least for the upper and middle classes, prosperous. It is a period, moreover, which lies at a safe distance from the Crimean War and not within dimmest sight of the second Boer War. Young people, a dozen years hence, will think, "What a Golden —or shall we say, what a Silver-Gilt—Age! Let us exalt the second half of the nineteenth century as it lies, fat and sleepy, between 1853 and 1899. True, the Pre-Raphaelites were a group of dissatisfied young men but they hardly disturbed our belovéd period until the 'seventies. Darwin, no doubt, upset the young men in innumerable comfortable households, but again—Darwin had in the Blessed 'Sixties not a tenth part of Mr. Carlyle's influence; and the bishops were able to smile at the impious but absurd doctrine that men were descended from monkeys."

So will they muse and murmur, donning their smoking-caps and fondling their dundrearies, in those little islands of culture (or dilettantism) which will first peep above the subsiding flood of post-war plain-practicality and no-nonsense. But let those young men with their whiskers and whalebone, those young women with their croquet-mallets and smoking-caps, take warning at once, take warning from me who may then be unable to address them in person, that they are thinking too handsomely of the airless eighteen-sixties. Had I been a successful author to whose new book "everybody" had annually looked forward, I could refer my gentle reader to many printed pages which prove (if they have not long since become salvage) that religion is, as it always has been, the foremost of my interests and, in fact, that I habitually see everybody as "not only a taxpayer but an immortal soul." In consequence, kind reader, do not misjudge me if I say that no sooner had the Regency rakes and romantics died out than an appalling and uncanny blight of evangelicalism hung suspended above the rest of the Victorian era until human nature, in pure desperation, asserted itself in Oscar Wilde, Beardsley, and the Yellow Book.

Sometimes a publisher's list of long years ago may bring us the smack of a period just as rudely as the rich reek of seaweed and fish will announce that we have arrived at Oban or Plymouth; and that is my reason for directing your attention to the advertisements of a Scottish publisher, named Nimmo, which even now forlornly cry their crumbled wares from the back pages of a book that bravely rode forth into the world (as bravely as this little book, mild reader) in the year 1869. . . . Forgive me if I indulge for a few moments in happy meditation upon that magical date. In 1869, you see, there must have been quite a number of old gentlemen in the clubs, old blacksmiths and saddlers in our villages, who had fought at Waterloo. And of course the Great Exhibition, that climax of civilisation, had occurred only eighteen years earlier. You did not need to have achieved the solemn forties in order to remember the Great Exhibition and the incredible Crystal Palace. So-called veterans of the Indian Mutiny or the Crimean War were still too plentiful for curious observation. Let us remember, too, that women were "the Sex," that ignorant young wives endured wedding-night martyrdom in their tens of thousands, that men regarded women as either baggages or angels, and that the doom of the unmarriageable girl was dire. . . .

But allow me to introduce you to Mr. Nimmo's astonishing catalogue. He had launched, for example, a *Library Edition of the British Poets*, and, mindful of our present passion for Mr. T. S. Eliot, Mr. Auden, and Mr. Dylan Thomas, I invite your consideration of Mr. Nimmo's poetic tips. "Shakespeare and Surrey" are bedfellows in "one vol." Goldsmith and Collins have to carry "T. Warton" on pick-a-back in their dash for the Parnassus Stakes. We are therefore the more surprised that the Reverend Mr. William Bowles, whose vogue we fancied had expired with *The Keepsake*, should be accorded the high tribute of being in "2 vols." The omniscient reader may disdain me (nor can I defend myself) when I admit to total ignorance of the poetic heights achieved by "Armstrong, Dyer, Green," whose labour Mr. Nimmo was able to compress within one volume. Another of his ventures—a most eccentric four-in-hand, or so does it seem in 1943—begins with the snorting name of "Johnson" (presumably, the Doctor), shamelessly proceeds to "Parnell," whoever he may have been, gathers charm with the name of Gray, and completes the equipage, a little surprisingly, with "Smollett."

These, however, were merely the Nimmo singing-birds. Mr. Nimmo made his money—it looks like an enviable fortune —out of the well-nigh universal piety and pale preoccupation with heaven which, despite our magnificent free trade offensive, seems to have characterised most of the population. There were, for example, the immensely popular works of Norman Macleod, D.D., who wrote *The Old Lieutenant and his Son*, *The Earnest Student* and (in part) *Across the River: Twelve Views of Heaven*. *Bell's Messenger* said of the last-named volume that "A more charming little work has rarely fallen under our notice, or one that will more faithfully direct the steps to that better land it should be the aim of all to seek." Those who, perhaps prematurely, were more concerned than Mr. Nimmo with the Better Land could at a very reasonable price acquaint themselves with what they might expect. *Heaven our Home* cost only eighteenpence, and one hundred thousand copies had already been purchased by would-be emigrants. No wonder! The book, we learn from the *Glasgow Herald*, "demonstrates the interest which those in heaven feel in earth, and proves, with remarkable clearness, that such an interest exists not only with the Almighty and among the angels, but also among the spirits of departed friends." A rival treatise called *Life in Heaven* ("twenty-first thousand," cries Nimmo, less diffidently than the subject calls for), was said by no less a paper than *The Cambridge University Chronicle* "to put before its readers such an idea of the reality of our existence there, as may tend to make a future world more desirable and more sought for than it is at present." And if anybody was still so gross as to be interested in earthly matters he—or she—had little or no excuse. Mr. Nimmo, always intent upon the better land, held out to him the "Sunday Evening Book," *Personal Piety* and *The Graver Thoughts of a Country Parson* (thirteenth thousand); and the reader of *The Eclectic Review* would find that Sarah Tytler's *Papers for Thoughtful Girls* was "one of the most fascinating books we

have ever seen for the rising youth of the fair sex." No book-
seller, I suppose, would have raised an eyebrow if some young
gentleman, born (say) in 1845, had asked for *The Earnest
Student* and *Papers for Thoughtful Girls*; and in view of so active
an effort to popularise heaven, it is surprising that our grand-
parents, even in the headiness of wild youth, should so far have
forgotten themselves as to produce our parents. The constant
thought of heaven may, perhaps, lead to some absence of mind.

This England, then, or this Scotland, was intolerably
frowsty. Nobody ever slept at an open window. Most windows
were in fact never opened at all. And there is no need to envy
the high-spirited maidens, born in the later 'forties, who were
conventionally supposed to be pining at twenty for the superior
pleasures of heaven. "To make a future world more sought for
than it is at present" was an ideal which pullulated such a fetid
mass of hypocrisy as no subsequent period could adequately
imagine; and yet it was into such a top-hatted and many-
petticoated society that Swinburne's *Poems and Ballads*, im-
ploring unheavenly women to "redeem us from virtue," had
recently exploded.

II

Now, all these flavours of the eighteen-sixties have been
captured and recorded from a book by that very Alexander
Smith at whose undramatic poem, "A Life Drama," Leon M.
Lion and I had made merry on a summer evening in less
murderous times. Allow me, long-suffering reader, now
belatedly to make amends and to persuade you that Alexander
Smith was by no measure a coxcomb or an ass. Here at Cambridge where the days have a drawling utterance and where
visitors rarely beguile the hours, I explored deeply into the
prose and poetry of a young man who, at first, as the retentive
reader will recall, was almost suffocated with the roses of praise.
Suddenly chilled by a dread lest some similar eclipse might
befall Eliot, Auden, or Dylan Thomas, I suspected that Smith
could not subsequently have merited quite so strong a dose of
oblivion's poppy; and before long I found myself increasingly
right.

Clearly, you will not be charmed by the man himself (as, in the end, I believe you will be) unless I can first indicate, however superficially, that Smith had some small gift as a poet and also an ear for graceful prose which, if they had the skill and the will to match it, might vastly improve the hasty and over-confident work of many among our most famous contemporary authors: for it is not the new poets only who absolve themselves from the difficult labour of extracting the music which lies latent in the English language.

Poetry, somehow, becomes old-fashioned (if it is not of eternal stuff) more noticeably than prose, and that is why we ought first to appreciate my Smith as an essayist. What, in the name of literary courage—considering the writer's period—could be more admirable than Smith's cool assessment of the then-overpowering historian, Lord Macaulay? "The World," says Alexander, "as it figures itself to Lord Macaulay, was a comparatively commonplace world. He cared for man, but he cared for party quite as much. He recognised men mainly as Whigs and Tories. His idea of the universe was a Parliamentary one." Compared with the way in which any real poet sees it, the world was indeed a "commonplace world" to Macaulay, just as it remains commonplace to nearly all members of parliament and all lawyers.

Again, not even Leigh Hunt's latest biographer has offered the running reader a more brilliant nutshell account of Hunt's undeniable, though somewhat invertebrate, charm than Smith has provided in the following sensitive passage. . . . "Leigh Hunt was a poet as well as an essayist, and he carried his poetic fancy with him into prose, where it shone like some splendid bird of the tropics among the sober-coated denizens of the farmyard. He loved the country; but one almost suspects that his love for the country might be resolved into likings for cream, butter, strawberries, sunshine, and hayswathes to tumble in. If he did not, like Wordsworth, carry in his heart the silence of wood and fell, he at all events carried a gillyflower jauntily in his buttonhole. He was neither a town poet and essayist, nor a country poet and essayist; he was a mixture of both—a suburban poet and essayist. Above all places in the world, he loved Hampstead. His essays are gay and cheerful as suburban villas—the piano is touched within, there are trees and flowers outside, but the city is not far distant, prosaic interests are ever intruding, visitors are constantly dropping in."

By this time I like to assume, unhurrying reader, that, if we were sitting *vis-à-vis* by this Cambridge fireside, you would fill up another pipe or, it may be, pick up another matter for stitchery, and encourage me to quote again. Well, then, will you not agree that this is well said and might have been said by the more successful Robert Louis Stevenson? I pray you, lend me your ears. "A quick ear and eye, an ability to discern the infinite suggestiveness of common things, a brooding meditative spirit, are all that the essayist requires to start business with." . . . (Stevenson would have said to commence author) . . . "Jacques, in *As You Like It*, had the makings of a charming essayist." And when I come to *Smith on Chaucer*, as the lawyers might say, I hardly know where to stop or at what point, invisible reader, your jigging right foot might notify impatience or your lifted left eyebrow suggest a wandering attention—so buoyantly does my Smith seem to call up the most attractive aspect of the fourteenth century. "The fourteenth century," he tells me, "loved magnificence and show. Great lords kept princely state in the country; and when they came abroad, what a retinue; what waving of plumes, and shaking of banners, and glittering of rich dresses! Religion was picturesque, with dignitaries and cathedrals, and fuming incense, and the Host carried through the streets." . . . Is it not all coming back to you—the colour and liveliness and pictorial genius of that age when Englishness had begun to push itself through the Frenchness of the very Court? But I must not permit myself, in mere enthusiasm, to interrupt the voice of my admirable Smith.

"London," he says, "is already a considerable place, numbering, perhaps, two hundred thousand inhabitants, the houses clustering close and high along the river banks; and on the beautiful April nights the nightingales are singing round the suburban villages of Strand, Holborn, and Charing. It is rich, withal; for after the battle of Poitiers, Harry Picard, wine merchant and Lord Mayor, entertained in the city four kings—

to wit, Edward, king of England, John, king of France, David, king of Scotland, and the king of Cyprus—and the last-named potentate . . ." (who would not happily accept the crown of Cyprus?) . . . "slightly heated with Harry's wine, engaged him at dice, and being nearly ruined thereby, the honest wine merchant returned the poor king his money, which was received with all thankfulness. There is great stir on a summer's morning in that Warwickshire castle—pawing of horses, tossing of bridles, clanking of spurs. The old lord climbs at last into his saddle, and rides off to court, his favourite falcon on his wrist, four squires in immediate attendance carrying his arms, and behind these stretches a merry cavalcade, on which the chestnuts shed their milky blossoms."

There's the true flavour of Chaucer's England, there's the fourteenth century as it seemed to its lucky inhabitants. Do not prate to me of the serfs and their rheumatical hovels, or prattle of medieval sewage, or fatuously assure me that Chaucer would have been happier if he had driven a motor-car. It is better to have rheumatism and an exciting religion than to have neither, and I for one would put up with bad drainage and an earlier death if I could be sure of daily pageantry and a gay-coloured singing London.

Let us hurry past the essay on "Mr. Carlyle at Edinburgh," for of all the over-rated and pompous bullies who somehow imposed upon the hero-worship of the Victorians Mr. Carlyle is the most pretentious and the hollowest. Let us overlook a certain timidity of judgment which misled Smith into writing "I really do not wish to advocate Ruskinism and the Gothic," as though "the Gothic" were a style not quite gentlemanly or an appreciation of it were merely a fashionable affectation. Smith, for all his merits, was no literary Columbus, no first announcer (as Gosse and Havelock Ellis were) of genius or high distinction not yet perceived by commonplace reviewers. Seeing that he himself was called a "spasmodic poet," Smith cannot have failed to read or to relish the brilliant, audacious, and newly published Poems and Ballads of young Mr. Swinburne, but he is content to advertise his acquaintance with the work of Tennyson and Browning: nor had he the intellectual fearlessness which enabled a few of his contemporaries to recognise that in Walt Whitman the world had found its most beautiful rhapsodist since the time of the early and unsophisticated Greeks or of the Old Testament prophets. Smith, indeed, like a hundred later essayists, fell a victim to the infectious mannerisms of Hazlitt. Were we busied over a parlour-game, suitable to so cold an evening of December; would the reader be quite certain, I wonder, whether it was Hazlitt or Smith or Stevenson or Montague who penned the following sophistical passage? "The playful capering flames of a newly kindled fire is a pretty sight, but not nearly so effective—any housewife will tell you—as when the flames are gone, and the whole mass of fuel has become caked into a sober redness that emits a steady glow. There is nothing good in this world which time does not improve. A silver wedding is better than the voice of the Epithalamium; and the most beautiful face that ever was, is made yet more beautiful when there is laid upon it the reverence of silver hairs." Hazlitt left the semi-colon a peril to all essayists, having invested it with a heavy weight of sententiousness.

It is when he forgets Hazlitt, and therefore ceases to sound like an uncanny anticipator of Robert Louis Stevenson, that Smith is so well worth rediscovery: for, alas, there is no permanent nourishment to be had from even the most skilful imitation of the most admirable models. There is genuine Smithness in "Ancient descent and glory are made audible in the proud murmur of immemorial woods;" in "Life has in many a patched and tinkered look;" and in the saying, ever-to-be-borne-in-mind, that "In every age public opinion is the disseminated thoughts of some half a dozen men, who are in all probability sleeping quietly in their graves." And while we are considering how strangely this nigh-forgotten author not seldom forestalled Stevenson, the reader, curious as any Ming mandarin in these literary minutiæ, will agree that Smith seems also, somehow or other, to have written like Richard Jefferies before Jefferies was able to spell out his name. Who will not recognise a passage in *The Story of my Heart* when he reads: "Love of trees and plants is safe. You do not run risk in your affections. They are my children, silent and beautiful, untouched by any passion, unpolluted by evil tempers; for me they leaf and flower themselves. In autumn they put off their rich apparel, but next year they are back again with dresses fair as ever; and—one can extract a kind of fanciful bitterness from the thought—should I be laid in my grave this winter, they would all in spring be back again with faces as bright and with breaths as sweet, missing me not at all." And before we close up the books of his prose, I recommend you, indefatigable reader, to find by hook or by crook the finest essay that Smith achieved, an essay not too much be-Hazlitted and, on the contrary, fit for inclusion in any anthology of English prose which ever shall be compiled by any wide-roaming editor—a paper, too, with a lovely and most surprising conclusion—that is to say, "A Lark's Flight."[1]

III

While I still wear my sackcloth of repentance, I must make some amends for having merely derided the poet in Alexander Smith, for although his life was short he considerably improved upon the youthful grandiloquence which seemed at first to have placed him among the major poets. If we remember that he lived mostly in Glasgow and Edinburgh (and he wrote a poem about each of these cities), we may catch a glimpse of the man and his place and his period when we read:

> The other night I lay within my bed,
> Watching my dying fire: it mouldered out.
> I listened to the strange nocturnal cries:
> A ballad-singer 'neath my window stood,
> And sang hoarse songs; she went away, and then
> An oyster-man came crying through the streets;
> And straight, as if I stood on dusky shores,
> I saw the tremulous silver of the sea
> Set to some coast beneath the mighty moon. . . .

Is that old-fashioned? It is—I confess it is, for what Auden

[1] About thirty-five years ago Smith was still faintly remembered by his prose-book *Dreamthorp*. He seems last to have excited some interest with *A Summer in Skye*, which is, indeed, a work to respect, but one that must necessarily have more attraction for Scotsmen than for the ordinary members of the human species.

or Day Lewis would write the word "'neath"; but is it not at all the more surprising that this poet, destined to dip his pen (as it were) so often in the inkpots of posterity, should have composed a stanza which may remind us of a poet named Rupert Brooke who was not due to write verses until another fifty years had gone by. There are still aged and infirm persons who recall the lines (by Brooke):

> I jumped to feel how sharp had been
>   The pain when it did live,
> How faded dreams of Nineteen-ten
>   Were Hell in Nineteen-five,

but would they not assent to a suggestion that Smith, writing in 1856, did somewhat better with the same theme? Thus:

> I cannot say, in Eastern style,
> Where'er she treads the pansy blows;
> Nor call her eyes twin-stars, her smile
> A sunbeam, and her mouth a rose.
> Nor can I, as your bridegrooms do,
> Talk of my raptures. Oh, how sore.
> The fond romance of twenty-two
> Is parodied ere thirty-four!

This, however, is but second-rate Praed, and Smith will turn over more comfortably in his grave if we read and examine five of the stanzas addressed to Edinburgh, for these are sensitively wrought and have the specific imagery of verse that has glowed into poetry.

> Within thy high-piled Canongate
> The air is of another date;
>   All speaks of ancient time:
> Traces of gardens, dials, wells,
> Thy dizzy gables, oyster-shells
>   Imbedded in the lime—
> Thy shields above the doors of peers
> Are old as Mary Stuart's tears.

> Street haunted by the step of Knox;
> Darnley's long, heavy-scented locks;

Ruthven's blood-freezing stare:
Dark Murray, dreaming of the crown—
His ride through fair Linlithgow town,
    And the men waiting there
With loaded fuse, undreamed of—wiles
Of Mary, and her mermaid smiles!

Thou saw'st Montrose's passing face
Shame-strike the gloating silk and lace,
    And jeering plumes that filled
The balcony o'erhead; with pride
Thou saw'st Prince Charles bare-headed ride,
    While bagpipes round him shrilled,
And far Culloden's smoky racks
Hid scaffold craped, and bloody axe.

What wine hast thou known brawl-bespilt!
What daggers ruddy to the hilt!
    What stately minuets
Walked slowly o'er thy·oaken floors!
What hasty kisses at thy doors!
    What banquetings and bets!
What talk, o'er man that lives and errs,
Of double-chinned philosophers!

These stanzas—in fact, the whole poem, unfortunately not finished—are finer than that one wild rhapsody "Barbara," which, enshrined in *The Oxford Book of English Verse*, is all that most readers know of this man's brief life-work.

IV

"A Life Drama" is so extravagant as to deserve mockery, but it is better in a young poet to be magnificently absurd than to be safely tepid; and the sympathetic reader will comprehend my sense of having wronged Smith when he learns something about the man himself. Sheriff Nicolson of Skye has this, for example: "Of all men whom I have known that drew forth love as well as admiration, Alexander Smith was the most lovable. It was impossible not to love him—as impossible as it was to provoke him to do or say anything mean or unkind. Unlike many whose whole goodness and fine sentiment is put into their books, his life and character were as beautiful as anything he wrote." Let us, then, throw a brief film of his life upon the screen of imagination. It will certainly lead us to like him.

Our hero was born at Kilmarnock, Ayrshire, on the last day of December, 1829, and, except for a slight cast in one eye, he was endowed with the Ayrshire good looks. His mother was a certain Helen Murray; his father was a lace-pattern designer. When Alexander was a child, the family moved first to Paisley and then to Glasgow. The lad, after a superficial schooling, followed the somewhat uncommon trade of his father, but he must have been one of those innumerable Scots who find time to read omnivorously because they are constitutionally incapable of living a boorish life. By the time that he was twenty, Alexander had seen some of his verses printed in "The Poets' Corner" of the *Glasgow Citizen*. A year later the Reverend George Gilfillan of Dundee, acclaiming the young artisan's talent before anybody had told him to do so, introduced Smith's verse to a somewhat larger public.

At this time, however, his dearest friend was a Scottish "character," an impassioned lover of poetry, an eager amateur botanist, named Hugh Macdonald. This Hugh was, no doubt, a salutary influence, especially as the poet had an inborn bias toward the vague and grandiose. "Keats," according to Hugh Macdonald, "was a puir bit penny-whistle o' an English cratur"; Shelley was "whiles bonny, bonny; but just clean daft, puir fellow"; and "o' him ye ca' Wudsworth," pronounced the Northern critic, "I hae just nae opeenion ava. He drank naething on' his life but Lake watter, they say; an' troth I weel believ't, for little else e'er cam' oot o' him." But the point is that during Smith's first blaze of glory (not paralleled even, I surmise, by that of Stephen Philips, another of Kit Marlowe's tribe), this candid friend was not to be shaken into applause. "I like ye weel, Sandy," said Hugh, "an' that ye weel ken; but as for yer poetry (as ye ca't) sae help me God! I mak' but little o't. It *may* be poetry; I'm no sayin' it is na; but it's no *my* kind of poetry. Jist a blather o' braw words, to my mind, and a wee bit whirly-whas, they ca' eemages! Damme if I can mak' either head or tail o't."

It was at the end of 1852 that Alexander Smith actually met with that golden experience of which every boy-poet dreams but which befalls not more than two or perhaps three young poets in the course of a whole century. A publisher of London, a Mr. David Bogue, issued Smith's poem "A Life Drama," giving him a hundred pounds for the copyright. The reader already knows the delirious and bacchic reception which this book obtained from the Press. Matthew Arnold, Kingsley, and Mrs. Browning discerned the exuberant promise of that book. Rossetti and Tennyson are said to have cared less for it, but we know that Tennyson—the laureate and high priest of literature in 1852—took the trouble to write a letter to Smith.

Heady with his hundred pounds, the young poet abandoned pattern-designing, and visited London accompanied by that John Nichol who subsequently became Professor of English Literature in Glasgow University. In London they met Miss Martineau—now, perhaps, a dim daguerreotype in the album of old renowns—and Lewes and Herbert Spencer and Samuel Helps. On the way home, they visited the Duke of Argyll. In 1854, finding that poetry does not pay, Smith was lucky enough to become Secretary of Edinburgh University. It was at this period (he was only four-and-twenty) that he met the formidable Mr. Ruskin at an academic banquet in Glasgow. Smith, never (I think) a killjoy of the bottle, said wildly that Mr. Millais' picture, "The Order of Release," was remarkable because the face of the woman expressed three emotions. To this Mr. Ruskin, sitting opposite, riposted with "Would you be good enough to let us know *distinctly*, Mr. Smith, *what* are these three emotions you speak of?" But poor Smith, paralysed by the boa-constrictor, had already lost count and could offer no reply.

In this year the poet Sydney Dobell made his temporary home in Edinburgh, an incident of note because Dobell was soon to be damned together with Alexander Smith as "poets of the Spasmodic School."

Three years later (1857) Smith married a damsel from Skye, her name being Flora Macdonald. His little book, *City Poems*, was now published, but with a result which would have embittered a less level-headed spirit. The attack upon Smith and Dobell was launched by a jingling ballad-rhymester, highly esteemed in his day, a flatulent and complacent word-spinner named Aytoun. This creature, manifestly incapable of any but pale emotions and respectable enthusiasms, went to the length of writing an immense review of a "spasmodic" poem ("Firmilian") by a non-existent poetaster, and then of actually taking the trouble to fabricate the poem. One of Smith's biographers speaks of Aytoun's "delightfully ludicrous Parodies," and makes the comfortably donnish remark, "I do not think anyone more heartily than Smith himself—with his abundant sense of humour—joined in Aytoun's laugh at his expense, and that of his friends." "A Life Drama" may be silly, but it is clearly the out-gushing work of a passionate, poetic, and deadly serious young mind. Only a don, or possibly a Fellow, could fancy that young authors appreciate the fun when they are made ridiculous in public.

After his marriage, Smith spent much of his time in Skye with, of course, the mother of his children. In 1861 he published a long blank-verse poem which was killed stone dead by the publication of Tennyson's *Idylls of the King*. Needing money, he turned to prose. In 1863 *Dreamthorp* appeared, that book of well-written essays which, according to one of his old friends, "contains most of himself." Two years later he edited the poetical works of Robert Burns, and put forth his still-pleasant but somewhat desultory book, *A Summer in Skye*. He now began to fancy that in Skye he might turn himself into a successful sheep-farmer—this man who, some ten years earlier, had been hailed as "better than Keats." Towards the end of 1866 he caught typhoid and diphtheria. He died on January the 5th, 1867, and was buried in Warriston Cemetery, near Edinburgh.

His rocket-like career, ending in a fallen and forgotten stick, must always make Alexander Smith attractive to the lover of fairy-stories from real life. He wore the full crisping beard which is said to have been popularised when our soldiers came back from their cold campaign in Russia—and is it not an awful reflection that Russia may have been the ultimate cause of W. G. Grace's great black beard, the most famous beard since that which the King of Spain found impudently singed? And the poet had a wide brow, curling hair, attractive and regular features. He was, they say, indifferent to politics, being doubtless unable to sustain an interest in them. Darwin's revelation seems not to have disturbed him, unless a refusal to talk about "metaphysics" (in other words religion) cloaked a scepticism concerning the very existence of Mr. Nimmo's "better land": but it is a little surprising that any poet, other than Rossetti, should have taken no interest in the American Civil War.

Despite the testimony of his friends he cannot, I believe, have been really stimulating company; but then, as a rule, the better the writer, the poorer the companion, for the men who write best are, like Shakespeare, listeners and not, like Jonson, talkers. I find that he did not answer letters, not even if they came from men who were famous: an attribute or defect which I cannot admire; and if it is true that "he would light his pipe with any paper from his pocket," we may have come to the origin of that report (of his having lit his pipe with a letter from Tennyson) which burned his name upon my memory when I was a boy running wild in the forest of literature. Indeed, one of his old friends, writing a panegyric, unguardedly drops the phrase "a man so quietly self-centred as Smith," and that impression is, I think, intensified by this old verbal snapshot: "Sunk in his easy chair, the Poet would placidly sit, beaming on his friends a quiet kindliness, and vomiting volumes of smoke upon them . . . his whole soul lapped in easy, indolent delight."

V

It is faintly conceivable that some person more liverish than the eupeptic reader might say to us, "Was it really worth while to dredge for the prose and verse of a second-rate writer whose work has not been reissued for at least a generation? Are there not numbers of far more talented authors who claim our besieged attention and our exiguous time? Come, come— there's no room in this packed century for any work but the best, the very best." But who is to tell us which writers are "the best"? It is certain that, if we should apply this cruel standard, we must remain almost entirely unacquainted with the authors who are now breathing; for experience assures us that out of all the writers in any generation or half-century, not more than five or six—and that is the highest possible number—will still be breathing, as it were, when the writers of two subsequent generations have hungrily trod them down. As well deny yourself the pleasure, then, of reading Mr. Sitwell or Mr. Sassoon as reject Alexander Smith because he predeceased them by a hundred years.

In 1860 English literature was leapingly alive. Anyone easily could name a dozen writers, then flourishing, who were widely famous and uncommonly skilled. More than a dozen, no doubt, are still diminishingly remembered, but not a dozen—not a half-dozen—are now genuinely current. First, your successful writer, such as Ruskin or H. G. Wells, George Eliot or Arnold Bennett, has only to produce a book and "the world" will promptly read it. Next, he continues to be a household name, but only three or four of his many volumes are read. At the third stage, none but professors or schoolchildren (as in the case of Scott) turn over the pages of perhaps a single work. Last stage of all in this eventful and characteristic history is a name in an encyclopaedia or else it is mere oblivion.

Ruskin, despite the many-faceted glory of his prose, is now almost in the state of a lean and slippered pantaloon. Thackeray is a wasted shadow, Carlyle, a dead and reeking tiger. Dickens had, it seems, a gift of immortality which must always puzzle the judicious—and so might we almost endlessly murmur the names of Victorian writers with whom Smith could have been acquainted; but when all have been cited and considered, we should possibly have to agree that only Tennyson and Trollope are now studied with passionate attention by those who are schooling themselves to be writers.

To some of us it seems flatly unthinkable that most of our living favourites will not be read at the turn of the century, and we have to pinch ourselves into recognising that it must be so. I can think at this moment of certain living poets whose work I would do much to save, if I could, for busy posterity, and it is with exasperation that I say to myself, "There will not be room for them." And perhaps a more practical man would not mind so much, for, after all, "we are like to the leaves' generations," and I have no doubt that the leaves are happy enough to feed upon sunlight and air and rain for the length of a spring and a summer, and are then content to spiral unnoticed to the earth. Smith (or at least my Smith) may not be "a name to resound for ages," and his most charming work may have lost some or all of its perfume, and yet we may grant to so kindly a man the humble immortality of an immortelle. If time is so different after death, perhaps he still cares.

XV

A PERFECT LIFE

I

IMMEDIATELY after the fire and flood at Albany my chattels were hurried down the old stone staircase and huddled all higgledy-piggledy into a grim and empty flat on the ground floor. The hose-water had made some of the furniture unrecognisable, and to look for any particular lar or penatis was a melancholy waste of time. Amaryllis's red shoes hobnobbed with glasses and a comely green decanter; evening-shirts and old batting-gloves stared up at me lugubriously from a shapeless mound of uncomfortable books; and the silk hat, worn by so many of my friends on their honourable progress towards Buckingham Palace, lay for weeks at a most undignified angle among dressing-gowns and manuscripts.

It was not until these and all things had at last been sorted out at Cambridge that I realised how this and that had incomprehensibly disappeared, and how two or three nigh-forgotten objects had turned up again—like little Greek relics in some vineyard of southern Sicily. And among these "objects" was a thin, blue, faded exercise-book (the price of "2d." still pencilled inside the cover) which I remembered at once as the diary of a friend who died—shot by a sniper—in the Four Years War. Now, it is only one year ago since I took a modest part in offering to the world a bundle of letters written by Bernard Shaw and by W. B. Yeats to the lady who, in 1912, bequeathed them to me; and it may seem a little odd that I should have inherited yet another intimate document—a diary, this time, and not an old letter-trove; but there it is, the occultists maintain that we attract what we most desire, and assuredly I have never read the autobiography of anyone, no matter how little he may have shared my delights, without speedily becoming absorbed in his tale, nor could I ever resist an old diary, even although it might contain only references to Papa as he loomed over the family in eighteen-sixty and to the mildest of meetings with a curate by the waterfalls of Bettws-y-Coed.

Of course, having so much less to do in Cambridge, especially as the darkening winter nights kept all Cambridge friends to their firesides, I re-read the little exercise-book, savouring its period taste and its human pathos without sentimentality because the past is my home-ground; and what is the passage of a mere thirty years to one who hobnobs daily with Borgia, Plato, and that irresistible eccentric, Ikh-n-aton? A young essayist has just informed his readers that I am "for all past time," and I call this uncommon handsome, but it might be truer to say that all past time is for me. The colour and music and brilliance of the princely establishments in Renaissance Italy have always precluded me from sharing my friends' enthusiasm for Switzerland or the Socialistic ideal; I realise with confusion and dismay that a slaveless Athens would have left no Dialogues, perhaps no *Antigone* and no *Clouds*, and certainly no European ideal of the perfectly balanced life.

I picked up S—— L——'s brief diary, therefore, somewhat as Duccio might have re-examined certain paintings by Margaritone—a man, I mean, whom he had known quite well, quite recently. Of necessity I have altered names and disguised places ("Bathsheba" is still alive, and so is "Jackie" if his luck as an airman still holds), but I can guarantee the reality of S—— L——'s unhappy pages. He had set himself to restore poetry to the London stage (I was following the same mirage), and had written at least two full-length Arabian Nights fantasies which had more merit and less fortune than the contemporary *Hassan* of James Elroy Flecker. Imagine my friend, then, as a well-to-do young man in a well-to-do period, married for about five years, and a father; but, as you will see, carried far beyond his depth by a romantic idealism which could hardly affect the more knowledgeable young people of the present time. I could not help thinking as I followed this day-to-day story how deftly Turgeniev would have transmuted it into a work of art. That is why I have chosen for it a title which the master might have approved.

II

March the 18th (1913)

During the last nine months my life has completely changed. A year ago I was happy—in a kind of sleepy way. I was married; I had a charming home; I was fond of Geraldine; and there was our baby—Jackie. I thought that all this would merely ripen during the next fifty years, like the pear-trees which Geraldine so optimistically planted when we came here, and that first she and then I would drop like ancient fruit from the tree of the world. In fact, I supposed that romance and adventure were for me henceforth only a memory.

In the March of last year I must have looked like a man who was emphatically "settling down," and we know what *that* means—death at the root! Why, once when I went up to London, friends exclaimed at my "stoutness" (I am twenty-five) and said that I had acquired a "farmer's walk." And then suddenly, last June, Bathsheba came to the Dower House—at Geraldine's invitation—and stayed three days and transfigured my whole life. Is it possible that nothing would have happened if G. had not gone up to London on legal business? We can't be such Fools of Chance. The world's great lovers must always have lain, like philippines, in the nutshell of Time.

Otherwise what can have made me anticipate her visit with such vibrancy of spirit? I remember so well how I went to meet her at W——, our nearest station. On occasions like this we hire what Geraldine calls "the pillbox," an antiquated form of doctor's conveyance, let out by the local butcher: and as it rumbled along the dusty roads I kept on thinking that the most beautiful human being whom I knew was coming to stay in my house. Great physical beauty does seem to me as holiness seems, I gather, to the Christians. The Athenians knew what I have in mind—that such exceptional loveliness of form is not a fluke but a translucent image of something in the world of perfection; and yet, of course, Bathsheba—half-English, half-Spanish—differs considerably from the classic ideal. There's much more fire, passion, and romantic burning-of-boats in her face than in the face of the Milo Venus.

On the platform at W—— I saw her. She was wearing a light summer frock, the colour of cornflowers, and a transparent large straw hat, and she was not unbecomingly freckled by the summer weeks that had gone.

As we drove back to the Dower House we were a little shy, but may that not always be so when the soul is upon the verge of some fundamental change? As soon as we arrived, she was charmed, as everybody is, by the Tudor graciousness of this old building, and particularly by the long, many-beamed attic that runs from end to end of the house, under the stone tiles. We lingered there for some time, looking down upon the plum-tree beside the porch and the two trim lawns with their three-sided border of "sceptral" lilies. . . .

Then there was the afternoon when we went for a walk through the unpeopled fields, and lay down in the long, seeding grass, far away from the whole world; and after a long silence, not having meant to say anything significant, I did say to her, "Don't expect to find a greater happiness in marriage than you can find in a deep friendship." She did not answer, but I could hear my words vibrating through her dark and mysterious mind. We had no intention of becoming lovers, and infidelity to Geraldine had simply not occurred to me as a possibility. But something had caught fire between us, and the impress of that hour and the glow of the evening that followed can never be obliterated from our memory.

After dinner we were sitting in the beamed music-room, and Lydia (the housemaid) brought lamps, and then Bathsheba went to the piano and sang in that soft, low, haunting voice two or three old, plaintive Russian folk-songs. I suppose she learned them when she was out there, three years ago. The warm tone of that voice and her southern exotic loveliness of line and colour awoke all the longing pent up within me, and for the first time we kissed, and it seemed that I was conjoined for those moments with all beauty—with the platonic Idea of Beauty—and simultaneously I knew that I was adventuring into a marvellous unknown country within which I had never meant to wander. I knew that our kiss would make us lovers and me unfaithful to Geraldine at least in heart, but what did all that seem to matter? I believe there's no ecstasy in nature to equal that of the moth as it flies into the flame.

She went away the next morning. I gave her a brown-golden rose—called, I think, Madame Ravary. Who, I wonder, was Madame Ravary? An enchantress? Or the hard-bosomed, money-minded wife of some typical Frenchman?

For weeks our secret remained happy and innocent. Occasionally, when I went up to London, we met for afternoon of meandering in Kew Gardens or Richmond Park. Bathsheba seldom spoke much, but Fate was as powerfully at work upon us as once upon Tristan and Isolde, Paolo and Francesca.

At the end of July Geraldine undertook a production of my old Egyptian play—written so long ago, five years ago! She liked Bathsheba. She asked Bathsheba to play a part in it; and day by day for a week in the Soho Rehearsal Rooms we hammered and stencilled and stitched. And once, under her breath, B. murmured one of those Russian songs.

Geraldine liked her so much as to take her for a holiday to Sark, and I was still so innocent of meaning to spoil our marriage that this arrangement did not seem at all bizarre. They came back, and from the moment of my welcoming them at the old oak door of the Dower House, our triple tragedy began. "I knew at once," said Geraldine, "that your welcome was not mostly for me." Can I really be so transparent?

For the last six days I have had to struggle with the problem of whether I should throttle the richest emotion which I have ever experienced, or break asunder from G.—from her who

looked to find everything in our marriage. Is there a harder
lot than to have to surrender the utmost beauty because it can
be obtained only at the cost of lifelong misery to another?
G.'s death is the sole solution that would exclude all suffering,
for if she lives and I remain with her I cannot possibly give
her a tithe of the love which she wants; and yet it looks as
though I must abandon my dream of a perfect life, and continue
here, year after year, with a torment of longing always falsifying
a façade of respectability and content.

I shall need to create an artificial personality. And youth
will pass, the loveliest of life will go by unfulfilled, unfulfilled.
I think I have always been enamoured of perfection, and
here, almost within my grasp, is the perfect life, and it has to
be renounced.

March the 19*th*

Every kind word or action puts another bond upon myself.
The happier I contrive to make her, the more remote becomes
my release. But it's useless to do anything half-heartedly, and
if that other love is to perish like a too brave flower in the
frost, I must do my best with what remains to me.

The papers are full of old Lord Roberts' warnings about
Germany. He urges "young Britons" to join the Territorials,
and I think I shall. After all, I love this Warwickshire country-
side, and we English, though dull, are a kindly lot on the whole.

March the 20*th*

After breakfast a long talk in the inglenook with G. Last
night I felt as though my constraint would send me mad. She
says that although she lives "in horrible pain all day," she still
wishes us to live together because of Jackie, and because she
would be even more unhappy if we lived apart.

In her position I should go away at once. No people ought
to marry without agreeing that the marriage need not be a
life-sentence.

March the 21*st*

How difficult it is to attain equilibrium. . . . The man who
forgets his own insignificance against the illimitable background
of Time and Space, is either ridiculous or pathetic; but the

man who is too conscious that "nothing really matters" is likely to prove ineffectual in the business of life. Human affairs are important on the scale of human existence, and, after all, it would be useless to see things as if you were not of human size. . . .

Yesterday at tea we had another talk. Like this. . . .

G. If you were free, would you marry her?

S. Yes, if it did not pain you. We could never be happy if you were in torment.

G. But you said a few weeks ago that you'd never marry again——

S. I said so in September because at that time Bathsheba and I had not been manœuvred into seeming to be guilty—of something!

G. Why don't you go abroad with her? She has often boasted that she doesn't care a fig for public opinion.

S. It would make you miserable; and I should know that, all the time.

G. Oh, you mustn't think so nobly. I can only keep you by being generous; and you change so quickly that I still have a hope that you may come to love me again.

S. It would be one thing to go away together for good, and quite another to spend a few weeks in Greece or Italy, and to return to the old conditions.

G. Do you want her physically?

S. I could easily forgo that.

G. If it is only her society that you want, ask her to come here. I know that nothing I have ever given you could equal the gift of her. . . .

What the devil is to be the result of it? It can't possibly end up happily for all of us. Will Fate bring Geraldine to an early death? And if Bathsheba and I were free, should we love always or would the light go out of us? If so—how grim and useless all this agony! I cannot go back a year in my feeling towards G., but at least I can cause her as little suffering as possible.

A few months before that marriage I wrote to her, in a clairvoyant hour, suggesting that I was not suited to marriage, too independent, not sufficiently philoprogenitive, and so on. To break then would have been hard, no doubt, but she has been happy for two years and to break now would be, I suppose, immeasurably harder.

March the 22nd

Last night we were talking about death. I said that I hated to read newspapers because somebody has always just died, and "the dead seem so out of it." "Oh, yes," she answered, "it seems so, no doubt, when you are happy." Happy! Evidently she realises nothing. Later, she said that she looked forward to death as "a new and thrilling life."

If she should die, I must not be tortured by a sense that I might have done more. I have done everything possible except to pretend a love that I don't feel: and she has implored me not to do that.

March the 23rd

It is difficult to remember the happy months of 1911, or rather, to recreate their happiness. They now seem burdened with latent thunder.

Looking back on our marriage, I think we never were very near in spirit. A woman's beauty of body was then a wonder, an excitement, which I did not know; and to every warm and vivid nature that first freedom of sex-fulfilment must be a mighty experience. It was for me. But the first glory of it all was over, I think, after about nine months, and mere physical delight is not enough to keep love alive in a man who is mostly imagination.

After tea, G. renewed her insinuations that Bathsheba has had a number of love-affairs in which she has "stopped at nothing." "Yes," I said, "she has certainly been much loved." "Evidently," replied G. The insinuations are rubbish.

In the end I told her that it was useless to talk about the situation any more. She must live with her regret for what is lost, and I with my sorrow for what might have been.

Thank heaven, I go away—to Spain—with three friends in a few days time.

April the 26*th*

Not having heard from B. for a fortnight, I left the others and rushed homeward. On the way I developed a violent fever —malaria, perhaps: and now I am in the grip of perpetual neuralgia.

April the 28*th*

It is painful to hear her making plans for the garden "next year," for it brings home to me the prospect of living imprisoned month after month, year after year, and the season of youth running out for us.

If I asked her to live apart from me I should be accounted cruel. If she went of her own accord, I should be accounted weak. The world says . . . oh, damn the world!

May the 2*nd*

[This entry is scrawled out—with the simple words "No good."]

> Bathsheba was golden-brown,
> Tall, fair and cool.
> She heaped her hair like a black crown,
> And stirred the rosy pool . . .
>
> *Oh, love, will you last?*
> *Oh, love, must you fade?*
> *Sweet are you, present, sweet when past;*
> *And I'll not be afraid.*
>
> David, king of that long line,
> Gazed—caught his breath—
> And cried, "O love, be you mine, mine;
> And I'll not care for death!"
>
> *Oh, love, will you last?*
> *Oh, love, must you fade?*
> *Sweet are you, present, sweet when past;*
> *And I'll not be afraid.*

May the 10*th*

Still no change. I have asked myself a hundred times whether I am behaving like a spoilt child—whether I ought to be able to "make the best of it." That's just the trouble— I don't believe that people should be reduced to "making the best" of life—in *that* sense.

Happiness comes from energy, energy from happiness. I am becoming lethargic, snow-buried under the weight of an unnatural life. Her life's happiness depends upon chaining me, mine upon freedom. One of us will have to give in—and I often feel tired out.

May the 30th

I stayed a few days with my mother in London. B. and I went to see two interesting plays: a novel production of *The Shrew*, with brilliant costumes by a man named Kruger, and a very strong play called *Typhoon*, by a Hungarian.

At supper (the Rendezvous, Dean Street) she questioned my belief that we ought not to give each other up entirely. Earlier, I had written to G., saying that I think we had better part. She replies that she could not possibly face living alone again, and would sooner kill herself. "Give me just half a hint, and I will do it now—while you are away." Of course I wrote to say "No."

When I got "home" (yesterday) she began by being very wan and melancholy. It is hard to discourage her from this death-idea because in doing so I have to fight against my own chance of liberty.

I do not know whether she means us to go on living in this emotional paralysis or to kill herself when I am off guard. Meanwhile I have to pretend to be light-hearted and aware of nothing. My nerves are certainly frayed.

June the 1st

G. has gone to town, and I have spent a sunny day in the garden. I feel sorry that it should be such a relief to find myself here alone.

I am not superman enough to believe that my life is worth the sacrifice of hers: and yet, looking at the problem squarely, it seems that I am doomed to sacrifice *my* life for the benefit of *hers*. Who can be blamed for loving one person more than another?

H.C. says, "Don't join the Terriers. You'll be an officer, naturally, and if there's a war you won't have a dog's chance." I suppose he's right, but I'm going through with it.

June the 12th

A year ago she came back with me in "the pillbox" from W——. Life in the country is only bearable when all is harmonious within. How long will Geraldine accept this ghastly travesty of married life? When she appears to assume that it is to continue indefinitely, I feel that I can't bear it for a day longer; and when she hints at suicide, I feel that I've got to endure it world without end.

I wish she wouldn't use Jackie as a weapon of moral blackmail. Apparently she has "arranged" for "dear old Dr. A." to adopt him "if anything happens." Anyway, that can't be legally possible.

July the 9th

I wonder what old age is like and whether it is best to die before the happiness of being young has melted away?

July the 14th

Can I do better than I am doing? Perhaps I ought somehow to be content with the knowledge that there is so profound a love between Bathsheba and me, and to bend my will to making G. reasonably happy. "To-morrow and to-morrow and to-morrow"—I understand that now.

July the 21st

She has been telling horrible stories of what she alleges B. to have told her when they took that holiday together.

August the 25th, 7 p.m.

The worst time of all. G. had decided to shoot herself. I had to snatch away the revolver, and then to walk up and down the garden for something like two hours dissuading her —and all the while wondering whether the alternative is worth fighting for.

I'm so tired now that I can't write any more. She may be dead by to-morrow morning for all I know. . . .

August the 26th

For these three days I have been steeling myself for the sound of a shot. That damn'd revolver. . . . Now—so far as I can discover—she has abandoned her plan. And I must prepare for another month of this grinding strain.

"Dr. A.," it seems, has been asked to "take charge of Jackie."

It is solely for her sake—if I am honest with myself—that I want her to live. I am not at all sure that life can now give her much that's worth having. Life here for me is almost unendurable, and I've now had twelve months of wretchedness. Life away from me is, she says, impossible for her. All that she asks is "a little tenderness"—so I suppose that all my efforts through all these months have achieved nothing, absolutely nothing.

There are two spiritual facts which make a tragic end—of some kind—inevitable. First, my sense that I am not morally required to spoil my life, youth, happiness, and work simply because I happen to love another so greatly; second, her refusal to live apart from me.

She reproaches me violently with thinking of no one but myself . . . as though, if that had been true, I should have stayed here through a year of anguish. And haven't I had to stop her from setting me free?

11.30 p.m.

This seems to be the very end. I am to stay with her; and Bathsheba and I must bury our dream of a perfect life—for ever. I shall join up (Territorials), but I don't suppose we shall really be needed.

III

This kind of love-madness, familiar to Stendhal, is bound to seem somewhat fantastic and exaggerated in these times. Even so, few students of love will be surprised to learn that the two dream-encircled lovers did in the end dare all conventions and live together "in sin": but their immense hopes broke down when "Bathsheba," more natural and less romantic than she had believed, wanted a child. She married in 1922 or 1923. Geraldine died in a motor accident in France, about a year later.

Why do I trouble to "transpose" and print this immediate

account of a youthful woe? Measured against the two vast
wars which have spoiled the world since then, how small does
that bygone trouble seem! But it is a man's personal career,
not the impact upon it of world affairs, which we find fore-
shadowed in his horoscope; and for each man the glittering
universe is merely a background to the life which he is dreaming.

XVI

CAVIARE—OR THE GENERAL?

COLONEL Q——, an old friend, was visiting Cambridge
as a Military Examiner, and one night, after dinner at the
Arts Theatre restaurant, King Maynard's claret went to his
imagination and he began to vaticinate. We had already agreed
in our wisdom, that the Second World War would end a great
deal sooner than our statesmen or our newspapers desired us
to believe; and then it was that the Colonel observed blandly,
"I'm afraid, my dear fellow, that you'll never get back to those
London rooms of ours, if only because in the new world such
delightful refuges will not be permitted to exist." He continued
—his mind winking beadily at the brim—to assure me that
science would be the only live interest of humanity, and that
there would be a coarsening of tastes and, naturally, an almost
complete disappearance of religion. Obviously he looked forward to seeing our planet controlled by Washington, London,
and Moscow. The relationship of the sexes, he warned me,
would at last become unromantic and really sensible; privilege
would be swept away in a legislative night; the under-dog
would emerge from the odd position which his name describes;
and for all imaginable time the world would be run in the
interests and according to the tastes of the Average Man.

When the bottle was empty he slightly darkened his pro-
phecy. In next to no time, he said, the United States of Europe
and Great Britain would be sparring with some animosity,
partly over the trade potentialities of the United States of

Germany, partly over the dual control of the French and
Belgian ports which the two victors had undertaken at first in
so brotherly a spirit. A minute or two later he was foretelling
a tremendous Asiatic war between the Soviets and "the British-
American Federation"; but as this event was not due, according
to the Colonel, until "1990 or thereabouts," when I should be
a well-preserved hundred and four and the Colonel himself a
centenarian, we adjourned our consideration of it *sine die*, and
went our ways into the warm and bombless night.

As I walked through the avenue of Trinity's lime-trees, I felt
considerable disquiet at the thought of Science Triumphant.
We seemed already to have suffered grievously enough in the
sacred cause of that new Juggernaut named Science. Even if
surgery and medicine have prolonged our lives—usually, perhaps, to little purpose—I had to admit to myself that I preferred
good drama to good drains, and would sooner die at forty in
an age of the arts than outlive Methuselah in a period of
machinery and microscopes.

At the same time, this bent of personality enabled me to
face with more than mere equanimity the likelihood that all
Europe, most of America, and much of Asia, will soon be
pervaded by the mind and temperament of Russia. My left-
wing friends (some ninety-eight percentum of the total) were
eagerly looking forward to the delights of social equality, but
for me the attraction of Russia was due to the seeming fact
that most Russians are persons who take naturally to beauty
and therefore require, rather than "encourage," the arts. I even
wondered with summer-night optimism whether some actual
British Government might presently be stung by Russian
example into taking the arts quite seriously. It was at this point
in my perambulatory meditation that I suddenly remembered
a certain passage about the future of Russia which I had read
in the small hours of the night before. Here it is. "I incline
to think what I have long thought: that if there is any such
future for us, and I believe there is, we of the older European
nations will be nowhere when it comes. In existence—yes,
perhaps; but gone down. You see, we are becoming greybeards
already; while you in Russia are boys, with every mark of

boyhood on you. You, you are a new race—the only new race in the world; and it is plain that you swarm with ideas of precisely the kind that, when you come to maturity, may re-invigorate the world. But first, who knows what deadly wars?" How many readers, I wondered—how many omniscient "intellectuals," even—could guess that these words appeared in the second volume of *The Yellow Book*, that is to say, in July 1894?

Russia, then, may bring back to Europe beauty and serious-ness. The United States may contribute, as her speciality—what? Energy, I decided. Continuous energy would be their irreplaceable contribution to the Millennium. And we our-selves? Not humour, for the Russians can supply it in plenty and in a form, oddly enough, which is not dissimilar from ours. Steady common sense, coming rather from Aberdeen or Yorkshire than from Piccadilly? No. In the last resort Ameri-cans guide their actions by a sense which is almost identical. Was it possible, then, that Shakespeare's countrymen could have nothing unique to cast into that New World broth? Perhaps, I thought, we shall contribute a certain tolerance, a certain respect for personality and even for oddity, which is rare among convention-loving Americans and presumably rare among equality-loving Russians. I should like to have supposed that we might be the aristocrats of the new world, giving Americans and Russians what the Greeks, though outnum-bered, continued to give to the Romans, but fine culture seemed hardly to be our long suit.

The Era of the Average Man which was, as it seemed, approaching, would at last wipe out all social distinctions, and abolish all forms of luxury, and provide better conditions for the general. No humane person could fail to cheer the dawn of that era. Any tale of oppression, any book by a Hammond or a Webb, could rend my vitals—like those vultures who so perseveringly attacked the inconsumable liver of Prometheus. Was there a man with soul so dead as not to rejoice in the downfall of the local Colonel, the upjump of the local grocer? There could be no such monstrous creature; and yet, as an artist, I could not help secretly lamenting the imminent loss of many fair things. Dramatists and women, I mused, love inequality because it makes for colour, pageantry, and romantic changes of fortune; nor was I truly able to understand how any artist could, like Lesley Blanch, allow a fashionable communism to make her forget or not perceive that kings and queens are deep and immortal and necessary symbols within our own souls, not merely obsolete dummies. The soul of America is sick for lack of a crown.

However, according to Colonel Q——, all social distinctions, culminating in the King and the Queen of a country, were to be ironed out. I still dreamed that I might live to see the long-forgotten soul triumphantly demonstrated by Russian scientists; and that men, in consequence, would set up a new and noble religion, and learn to look more proudly at the huge and mindless mechanism of the universe that surrounds us, and that the word "soul" might again be used as unself-consciously as the word "heart" or "head." But I saw at once that so inspiriting a change could hardly occur because, if it did, H. G. Wells would have been bombinating, all his life, in a vacuum.

By the time that I had reached my Cambridge igloo, I had little hope left. My prayer to the stars overhead was, in fact, whittled away to a desperate plea that when the rise of the Average Man had swamped society, I might yet, by some miracle, see an end of that sentimental and degenerate cult of the Little Man. The Little Man has been glorified far too long; glorified by Wells, glorified by Chaplin, glorified—obliquely— by Walt Disney. Of course, all the millions of Little Men are delighted and make themselves a box-office "certainty." They have been flattered. They have been told that they are, essentially, the salt of the earth. Now, all of us know that these Little Men are pathetic and are occasionally capable of the finest heroism; but I pray, howsoever vainly, that Little Men may now be left to their native insignificance, and that we may see a much healthier cult of admiration for the Outsize Man— Xenophon, Leonardo, Sir Walter Raleigh, Lincoln, Tolstoy, or General Smuts—for the Little Men will never grow taller if he is assured from all sides, by films and by novels and by plays, that he is everything which the heart can desire.

For me there is comfort in the knowledge, derived from a love of history, that the expectations of the "intellectual" have sometimes proved as faulty as those of Old Moore. The future tends to surprise us: and so, although everybody around me is confidently predicting an era of uniformity and flatness, I shall continue to hope for an era (not in my time) of variety and splendour. After all, who, in 1793, could have foreseen the style and charm of the First Empire?